Why It's OK to Love Bad Movies

Most people are too busy to keep up with all the good movies they'd like to see, so why should anyone spend their precious time watching the bad ones?

In *Why It's OK to Love Bad Movies*, philosopher and cinematic bottom feeder Matthew Strohl enthusiastically defends a fondness for disreputable films. Combining philosophy of art with film criticism, Strohl flips conventional notions of "good" and "bad" on their heads and makes the case that the ultimate value of a work of art lies in what it can add to our lives. By this measure, some of the worst movies ever made are also among the best.

Through detailed discussions of films such as *Troll 2*, *The Room*, *Batman & Robin*, *Twilight*, *Ninja III: The Domination*, and a significant portion of Nicolas Cage's filmography, Strohl argues that so-called "bad movies" are the ones that break the rules of the art form without the aura of artistic seriousness that surrounds the avant-garde. These movies may not win any awards, but they offer rich opportunities for creative engagement and enable the formation of lively fan communities, and they can be a key ingredient in a fulfilling aesthetic life.

Matthew Strohl is Professor of Philosophy at the University of Montana. He received his Ph.D. from Princeton University and blogs about movies, food, and philosophy of art at strohltopia.com and aestheticsforbirds.com.

Why It's OK: The Ethics and Aesthetics of How We Live

About the series:
Philosophers often build cogent arguments for unpopular positions. Recent examples include cases against marriage and pregnancy, for treating animals as our equals, and dismissing some popular art as aesthetically inferior. What philosophers have done less often is to offer compelling arguments for widespread and established human behavior, such as getting married, having children, eating animals, and going to the movies. But if one role for philosophy is to help us reflect on our lives and build sound justifications for our beliefs and actions, it seems odd that philosophers would neglect arguments for the lifestyles most people—including many philosophers—actually lead. Unfortunately, philosophers' inattention to normalcy has meant that the ways of life that define our modern societies have gone largely without defense, even as whole literatures have emerged to condemn them.

Why It's OK: The Ethics and Aesthetics of How We Live seeks to remedy that. It's a series of books that provides accessible, sound, and often new and creative arguments for widespread ethical and aesthetic values. Made up of short volumes that assume no previous knowledge of philosophy from the reader, the series recognizes that philosophy is just as important for understanding what we already believe as it is for criticizing the status quo. The series isn't meant to make us complacent about what we value; rather, it helps and challenges us to think more deeply about the values that give our daily lives meaning.

Titles in Series:

Why It's OK to Want to Be Rich

Jason Brennan

Why It's OK to Be of Two Minds

Jennifer Church

Why It's OK to Ignore Politics

Christopher Freiman

Why It's OK to Make Bad Choices

William Glod

Why It's OK to Enjoy the Work of Immoral Artists

Mary Beth Willard

Why It's OK to Speak Your Mind

Hrishikesh Joshi

Why It's OK to Be a Slacker

Alison Suen

Why It's OK to Eat Meat

Dan C. Shahar

Why It's OK to Love Bad Movies

Matthew Strohl

Selected Forthcoming Titles:

Why It's OK to Get Married

Christie J. Hartley

Why It's OK to Mind Your Own Business

Justin Tosi and Brandon Warmke

Why It's OK to Be Fat

Rekha Nath

Why It's OK to Be a Socialist

Christine Sypnowich

Why It's OK to Be a Moral Failure

Robert B. Talisse

Why It's OK to Love Bad Movies

For further information about this series, please visit: www.routledge.com/Why-Its-OK/book-series/WIOK

MATTHEW STROHL

Why It's OK to Love Bad Movies

Routledge
Taylor & Francis Group
NEW YORK AND LONDON

Cover Image: Andy Goodman

First published 2022
by Routledge
605 Third Avenue, New York, NY 10158

and by Routledge
2 Park Square, Milton Park, Abingdon, Oxon OX14 4RN

Routledge is an imprint of the Taylor & Francis Group, an informa business

Library of Congress Cataloging-in-Publication Data
A catalog record for this title has been requested

ISBN: 978-0-367-40766-7 (hbk)
ISBN: 978-0-367-40765-0 (pbk)
ISBN: 978-0-367-80896-9 (ebk)

DOI: 10.4324/9780367808969

Typeset in Joanna MT Pro and DIN Pro
by codeMantra

To my brother Josh,
my bad movie partner since the beginning.

Contents

Acknowledgments

I am grateful to Andy Beck for instigating this project and helping to bring it to fruition, and to Thi Nguyen for his matchmaking instincts and for everything else. John Dyck was the first person who got me thinking philosophically about bad movies and our many discussions about the topic have influenced every aspect of the book. I have also benefited from discussions over the years with many other friends and colleagues, including, but not limited to, Zed Adams, Aderemi Artis, Dave Baker, Aleksey Balotskiy, Elizabeth Cantalamessa, Jacob Collins, Ley Cray, Anthony Cross, Anne Eaton, David Friedell, Keren Gorodeisky, Sterling HolyWhiteMountain, Alex King, Colin Klein, Robbie Kubala, Dominic McIver Lopes, Eric Marcus, Aaron Meskin, Brian Montgomery, Shelby Moser, Jozef Müller, Alexander Nehamas, Stephanie Patridge, Brandon Polite, Geoff Pynn, Nick Riggle, Guy Rohrbaugh, Francey Russell, Elizabeth Scarbrough, James Shelley, Nick Stang, Christy Mag Uidhir, Servaas van der Berg, Ara Vartanian, Nicholas Whittaker, and Mary Beth Willard.

I am grateful to participants in Camp Aesthetics 2019 for helpful discussion. Thanks to James Harold for inviting me to discuss draft material with one of his classes at Mount Holyoke College, and to the students in that class for their lively and insightful contributions. My friend Ali Tabibnejad generously donated his services and formatted all of the screenshots found in the book. My colleagues in the Department of Philosophy at the University of Montana have been immensely supportive of my slow migration from Aristotle scholarship to writing about bad movies. I am grateful to my beloved wife Angela for finally coming around to Dolph Lundgren and for all that she's done to support me along the way. High fives to my main bad movie accomplices in life, Josh Strohl and Jesse Driscoll. Love and thanks to my mom Patti, my sister Alexis, my siblings-in-law Isabel and Mickey, my mother-in-law Suzanne, my niece Sky (who is already well on her way to becoming a bad movie lover), and my nephews Lachlan Bryan and Charles Bronson Strohl.

Finally, thanks to my dear, departed dad for raising me on the Cannon Group and for being so awesome. I miss you, old man.

The Good, the Bad, and the Good-Bad

One

When I was in graduate school, one of my roommates came home from a big exam that he had spent months studying for and said he wanted to watch a movie. I had something rented and asked him if he wanted to check it out. He responded: "No, that's too good. I need something much worse than that. Something really, really bad."

And I could relate! When I felt like he did after my own big exam I reached for Jon Amiel's 85 million dollar sci-fi extravaganza *The Core*. The film's premise is that the core of the Earth has *stopped spinning*. The planet's electromagnetic field is fading fast, and the apocalypse is nigh. Aaron Eckhart is dressed like a scientist and explains the situation with confidence and commitment. We'll all be dead in a year.

The only solution to this apocalyptic quagmire is to journey to the center of the Earth and detonate all the nuclear bombs at once to jumpstart the rotation of the core. But where will we find a vehicle that could tunnel through the outer mantle and withstand the extreme heat and pressure found within? No problem, just call in Delroy Lindo, who just so happens to have been holed up for years developing an appropriate ultrasonic laser along with a material that converts heat and pressure into usable energy. Lindo explains how he managed to devise such a miraculous substance: "I combined the crystals

DOI: 10.4324/9780367808969-1

in a tungsten-titanium matrix at supercool temperatures, and that's what did the trick." What did he name it? Unobtainium.

So the plan is to build a ship out of Unobtainium with the ultrasonic laser attached to the nose. But we also need a crack team, which will include Eckhart as the leader, Lindo as the tech guy, DJ Qualls as a skinny hacker whose job is to hack the entire internet to prevent anyone from finding out about the coming electromagnetic apocalypse (he demands unlimited Hot Pockets and *Xena: Warrior Princess* tapes to sustain him through his efforts), Hilary Swank as a NASA pilot who keeps her cool under pressure in spite of the prejudice she's encountered as a young female pilot, Stanley Tucci as an arrogant, well-dressed, world famous geologist (as though there is such a thing), and Tchéky Karyo as an overwhelmingly handsome French nuclear specialist.

Some of the cast know they are in a silly sci-fi adventure movie. But not Aaron Eckhart: he is deep in method acting territory. Looking forlorn at the horizon, which foreshadows the electromagnetic apocalypse with dramatic lightning storms and aurora effects visible at unheard of southerly latitudes, he snarls: "God, I hate this sky." Once the epic adventure is underway, several team members die. Eckhart really and truly feels each of their deaths. It's too much grief for one man to bear (image 1).

Is *The Core* a bad movie? In one sense, yes. Nothing makes *any* sense and yet it is all explained in a very authoritative tone. The utter silliness of the premise clashes with the dire seriousness of the drama. Eckhart's intensity is orders of magnitude out of step with everyone else's. I can recognize these elements as "bad." But they are exactly what I love about the movie, and they are the reasons I keep rewatching it instead of a conventionally "good" sci-fi movie. The straight-faced fake science

Image 1: *The Core* (2003) (Credit: Paramount Studios)

cracks me up. I find Eckhart's screaming tantrums so much more interesting than typical nondescript disaster movie lead performances. For me, at least, *The Core* is so bad that it's good.

***

But what does that even mean? How can a movie be good because it's bad? Aren't "good" and "bad" opposites?

It can't simply be that a movie that is bad enough automatically becomes good. There are plenty of movies at the far limit of badness that are simply boring or uninteresting. I recently watched the 2019 horror movie *Head Count*, for instance, and I thought it was just plain awful. It's derivative, dull, humorless, and tame. I found it extremely bad, but I never even considered the possibility that it's so bad it's good.

One thing seems evident: when we say a movie is "so bad it's good," or "good-bad," we are using the terms "good" and "bad" in different ways. We obviously don't mean that a movie is good in the exact same way that it's bad. Usually, when we say that a movie is good or bad, we mean to be rendering an overall verdict. Let's call this the *final* sense of the terms "good" and "bad." Saying that an artwork is good in the final sense means that one judges it to be *aesthetically valuable*, and saying that it is bad in the final sense means that one judges it to be *aesthetically disvaluable*. When someone says that a movie is "so bad it's good," they clearly don't mean that it's so bad in the final sense that it's good in the final sense. That would be nonsense. They must be giving one of the two terms a special meaning. There are at least two possibilities:

Bad Movie Ridicule: "Bad" is being used in the final sense, while "good" has a special meaning. "Good" means something like *ripe for mockery*. "So bad it's good" means that an artwork is bad in the final sense but that one still enjoys watching it, not because one judges that it's aesthetically valuable, but because one enjoys making fun of it.

Bad Movie Love: "Good" is being used in the final sense, while "bad" has a special meaning. "So bad it's good" means that one recognizes that there is some limited sense in which the movie is bad, but that one ultimately judges it to be aesthetically valuable, in part *because* it's bad in this limited sense.

I think the phrase "so bad it's good" is commonly used in both of these ways. First, let's focus on Bad Movie Love, which entails finding aesthetic value in movies that one recognizes are bad in some limited sense. Philosophers disagree about the nature of aesthetic value (to put it mildly), and we can't possibly settle the matter here, but I *do* have a theory. I'll sketch this theory in a moment, but for now let's try to be as neutral as possible and just say that a movie is good in the final sense if it's *worthwhile* and bad in the final sense if it's *not worthwhile*. That is to say, a good movie in the final sense is one that is worth our time and attention. When a Bad Movie Lover says that a movie is so bad it's good, they mean that the movie is bad in some limited sense, and because of this it's good in the final sense—it's worth our time and attention. But what is this limited sense of badness?

Philosophers John Dyck and Matt Johnson have proposed an analysis.[1] They think that the "bad" in "so bad it's good" denotes *artistic failure*. Artistic failure consists in an artist failing to achieve what they intend to achieve, which might happen at the stage of conception or execution. Returning to the example of *The Core*, we might say that it failed at the conception stage because the writers aimed to present a quasi-credible disaster scenario but the fake science they came up with is so absurd that the scenario is comical. We might also say that it failed at the execution stage because the film's silliness makes the dramatic scenes of Eckhart's despair and grief play as campy when they are supposed to be poignant.

Dyck and Johnson's view is that a movie like *The Core* can be *aesthetically valuable* in virtue of being an *artistic failure*. So when we say that *The Core* is bad, on their analysis we mean that it fails at its aims. When we say that it's so bad it's good, we mean that it fails at its aims in a way that makes it aesthetically valuable. In particular, they think that the baffling artistic choices that such movies manifest can give them a quality of *bizarreness* that we can appreciate aesthetically. Bizarreness is a quality that we often appreciate in movies such as *Mulholland Drive* or *Donnie Darko*, and so it's not surprising that we also enjoy it in movies like *The Core*. The difference is that the bizarreness of *Mulholland Drive* is clearly deliberate whereas in *The Core* it seems to be the cumulative result of the film's various failures. Indeed, *The Core* feels extra bizarre precisely because it's not supposed to be bizarre. Aaron Eckhart's acting choices are so strange in part because *he really means them*. But the fact that the bizarreness of *The Core* is not deliberate doesn't mean that we can't appreciate it aesthetically; it just means that we can't appreciate it *as a product of deliberate artistry*. We can enjoy the result without admiring the artistry that went into producing it.

Consider the way that we enjoy beauty in the natural world. When I see a beautiful sunset, I don't imagine that anyone created it with the intention that it be beautiful. Lots of things are like this. A tool that is designed with only functionality in mind might be aesthetically interesting to us because it reminds us of a medieval torture device and so comes across as a sort of horror sculpture. We don't need to imagine that its designer intended for it to remind us of a medieval torture device in order to find it interesting in this way. The Dyck–Johnson picture is that good-bad movies are intended to be good in one way, but miss the mark so widely that they turn out to be good in another, unintended way. We can admire a movie for its unintended bizarreness in much the same way that we can admire a sunset for its unintended beauty or a tool for its unintended horrifying quality. We can't attribute such a movie's aesthetic value to the artistic achievement of the artist, but we can nonetheless appreciate it aesthetically.

Dyck and Johnson's view is a good place to start, but I don't agree with their analysis. One problem they face is that a lot of titles that are traditionally included under the umbrella of good-bad movies are intended to be the way they are. Tom Green's good-bad masterpiece *Freddy Got Fingered*, for instance, succeeds at exactly what it's trying to do. It's a deliberate assault on standards of taste. Green knew perfectly well that chewing through an umbilical cord with his teeth and then swinging the baby around by the severed cord and splattering the walls with amniotic fluid would be beyond the pale (image 2). He knew that this would be so repulsive to the sensibilities of mainstream cultural tastemakers that they would reject it. This was the movie he wanted to make and the response he wanted to elicit. Back when it was first released, I remember cackling at the thought that Green was given 14 million dollars to make a movie and *this is what he did with it*.

Image 2: *Freddy Got Fingered* (2001) (Credit: 20th Century Fox)

Freddy Got Fingered was nominated for five Golden Raspberry Awards, or "Razzies." Razzies are parody awards given to the worst movies of the year in categories such as "Worst Picture" and "Worst Actor." Tom Green showed up to the ceremony with his own red carpet and declared: "When we set out to make this film we wanted to win a Razzie, so this is a dream come true for me." Eventually, he had to be pulled off the stage after accepting his award because he refused to stop playing the harmonica. He didn't fail at making a good movie, he succeeded at making a bad one, which suggests that a bad movie cannot be understood simply as a movie that fails at its aims.

Dyck and Johnson are aware of this objection and have a response. They think that deliberately bad movies are a separate category from good-bad movies and that we enjoy them in a different way. When we believe that a movie is deliberately bad, we think of its badness as an artistic choice and thus engage with it differently than in cases where we think that it fails at what it's trying to do. When I watch *The Core*, I enjoy Eckhart's performance partly because his emotional intensity is so out of step with the rest of the cast. If I thought he were deliberately trying to create the appearance of incongruous intensity, his performance would not be so delightfully baffling. I would think "oh, he's doing a shtick where he's much more serious than everyone else." It might still be amusing, but it wouldn't come across as absurd.

Dyck and Johnson are right that we sometimes engage with a movie differently when we think certain elements are intentional than we would if we thought they were unintentional, but I'm still not convinced by their account. There are two main problems. First, the possibility of intentional badness does not fit with their analysis of badness as failure, and, second, it is often not clear to us whether or not a movie's badness is intentional.

If badness were failure, what would it mean for a movie to be *intentionally* bad? It would mean that the movie intentionally creates the impression that it fails at something. But that's not what *Freddy Got Fingered* does. When Tom Green chews through that umbilical cord and then swings the bloody baby around by the severed cord, this does not create the impression that he's trying and failing to pull off a crowd-pleasing comedy gag that most people would enjoy. He's doing something similar to what John Waters did in movies such as *Pink Flamingos* and *Female Trouble*: freaking out squares and getting riotous laughs from audience members with transgressive taste. John Waters and Tom Green do not give the impression that they try and fail to meet mainstream standards. Rather, their work expresses disdain for these standards. Waters once said: "Taste is style, and to know bad taste of course you have to have been taught the rules of the tyranny of good taste so you can yearn to break them."[2] When Waters and Green made their films, they knew the rules and they deliberately trampled over them.

The other problem with Dyck and Johnson's picture is that we often aren't in a position to know whether some aspect of a movie is deliberate or not. Take Ridley Scott's widely panned 2013 film, *The Counselor*. In one scene, Benicio del Toro enthusiastically recounts an occasion when Cameron Diaz's character masturbated by straddling the windshield of his car in a full split and rubbing herself against the glass. We see a fairly explicit flashback. The movie as a whole has a serious posture and prestigious pedigree, with Scott directing a script from Cormac McCarthy. Some very upsetting things happen and they are presented with a heavy tone. But the movie also has scenes such as Diaz's windshield masturbation interlude that are so extravagantly ridiculous that the audience isn't quite sure how to take them. One is prompted to wonder: "Is this scene supposed to come across as absurd or did McCarthy intend for it to be in proportion to the rest of the movie and Sir Ridley just ran wild with it?" The fact that the baseline tone is heavy is what makes the masturbation scene (and Cameron Diaz's performance in general) so baffling. It's hard to tell if the jarring incongruity of this scene with other elements of the movie is intentional or not. If it were obviously intentional, it would just play as a joke, but because we don't know quite know how to take it, it becomes more than a joke. It gives the movie as a whole an eccentric quality. The film is outrageous, but also straight-faced, and we don't know how to reconcile this tension. This form of intriguing uncertainty is a common feature of our engagement with art, including good-bad movies (whether or not *The Counselor* in particular belongs in that category), and so we should reject the claim that we necessarily think of the badness of such movies as unintentional.

***

I have an alternative proposal. I've suggested that some good-bad movies are intentionally bad, others are unintentionally bad, and still others are ambiguous from the audience's point of view. The question we need to ask is what exactly it is that we think is intentional, unintentional, or ambiguous across the full range of cases. What is it that *The Core* does unintentionally and *Freddy Got Fingered* does intentionally? I propose that the answer to this question is *rule-breaking*. *The Core*, for example, appears to unintentionally break the rule that, other things being equal, all the acting performances in a movie should be on the same approximate wavelength. *Freddy Got Fingered* flagrantly and deliberately breaks all sorts of rules about the boundaries of good taste. *The Counselor* breaks a rule about continuity in tone by including a handful of outrageous scenes in a movie that is very serious in other ways.

But what are these rules and where do they come from? They're surely not written into the fabric of the universe. They often differ from culture to culture and era to era. I propose that we think of the relevant rules as *received norms*. A norm is a rule or standard, which may be informal and unstated.

"Don't pee in the pool" is a norm. There are norms concerning art, such as the norm that the mysteries in mystery novels should have coherent solutions and the norm that the boom mic should never intrude into the frame in a movie. A *received* norm is one that is taken for granted in a particular context. For our present discussion, the relevant context is mainstream critical discourse about movies. Received norms are the norms that can be appealed to in this context without need for further argument or justification. "Mainstream" loosely corresponds to the Rotten Tomatoes aggregate, especially the so-called "Top Critics" with regular gigs at major media outlets. There are certainly some critics on Rotten Tomatoes with outlier viewpoints, but part of the point of aggregating critical opinion is to drown these voices out and arrive at a "Critics Consensus" that is presented and received as the "Official Opinion."[3] To be clear, I am not saying that received norms are simply "what most of the critics think." Received norms are informal rules that can be invoked without further justification.

It will be helpful to consider a few examples of what it looks like when a critic appeals to a received norm:

Criticism 1: The story doesn't make sense. How did they get a boat? There is just no clarity at all about where this boat came from.

Norm 1: A narrative should explain major developments and not leave big gaps like failing to account for how the characters came into possession of a boat.

Criticism 2: The lead actress is really bad. She's supposed to be doing a Scottish accent but it actually sounds more like a cross between Klingon and Australian.

Norm 2: Accents should be realistic.

Criticism 3: The jokes are so crude that only a stoned college freshman could possibly find them funny. Do we really need to see a man chug a glass of horse semen? How is that a joke? I nearly lost my lunch. Not my idea of a good time at the movies.

Norm 3: Don't be *too* gross.

These are all criticisms that we might expect to find in a movie review in a mainstream publication. None of them requires further argument or justification. For Criticism 1, the critic does not need to go on to explain why it's a problem that the narrative has such a noticeable gap. It's taken for granted in the context that a gap of this sort is a flaw. Similarly, a critic doesn't need to give a further argument as to why an unrealistic accent or an especially disgusting joke is a defect.

If, in contrast, a critic were to present these aspects of the movies as merits, they would have some explaining to do, because their claims would be in tension with received norms. A film critic writing for the *New York Times* can't simply declare without further justification, "it's great, the narrative is full of holes" or "it's great, her accent is totally unrealistic," or "it's great, you've never seen anything so gross."

My proposal is that the when Bad Movie Lover says that a movie is so bad that it's good, "badness" should be understood as *conventional badness*. Roughly, "conventional badness" is badness according to received norms and standards. The Bad Movie Lover recognizes that a movie violates received norms and so is likely to get bad reviews and be widely disliked, but thinks that it is, in fact, good (in the final sense), and moreover thinks that it's good in virtue of the ways that it violates received norms. Not every conventionally bad movie is automatically so bad it's good. A movie can violate received norms by being bland, dull, and lifeless. Such a movie is just plain bad, not good-bad. Bad movies have the potential to be good-bad when they violate received norms in an exciting, interesting, and/or amusing way.

Conventional badness is not the same thing as failure, in Dyck and Johnson's sense. Sometimes the team making a movie tries but fails to adhere to received norms. In such cases, the movie is bad *because* of failure, but its badness does not *consist* in its failure. Its badness consists in the particular way in which it violates received norms. In this sort of case, norm violation is explained by failure. Other movies, like *Freddy Got Fingered*, don't attempt to adhere to received norms in the first place and so they cannot be described as *failing* to do so.

For someone whose aesthetic sensibility is thoroughly mainstream, conventional badness and final badness end up being one and the same. If someone has the same approximate taste as the Tomato consensus, the works that they find worthwhile will end up being the ones that meet conventional standards. Bad Movie Lovers, in contrast, find certain movies worthwhile in part *because* they violate these standards. They can recognize that there is some *limited* sense in which they are bad, but it's not the final sense. The way I often put it in casual conversation is: "I know what *you* mean by bad, and I agree that it's that, but I don't think it's bad."

Returning to my earlier examples of received norms, if I'm trying to explain why I love a conventionally bad movie, I might very well say things like:

"It's so wonderfully ridiculous. All of a sudden the characters have a boat but there's no explanation of where they got this boat from."
"The lead actress' accent is amazing! It's supposed to be Scottish but it sounds more like a cross between Klingon

and Australian. It's the most absurd accent I've heard in a movie since Nic Cage in *Captain Corelli's Mandolin*."

"It goes so far you won't even believe it. It doesn't just stretch the boundaries of good taste, it obliterates them. A guy chugs a glass of horse semen! A bunch of people walked out. You've gotta go see it."

The core of Bad Movie Love is the celebration of transgression and irreverence, and in this way good-bad movies turn out to be neighbors of the avant-garde. The term "avant-garde" applied to cinema is often used to narrowly refer to non-narrative films. Here I mean to use it in a broader sense that encompasses all sorts of experimental, boundary-pushing works, including some narrative films. Like the good-bad, the avant-garde is distinguished by its penchant for violating received norms. Indeed, the boundary between the good-bad and the avant-garde often looks pretty arbitrary. In a recent interview on the occasion of the 20th anniversary of the release of *Freddy Got Fingered*, Tom Green explained his intentions for the film:

> Well, I've always loved dark movies and strange films and, you know, I'm a big fan of David Lynch and David Cronenberg. I also love Monty Python and I love SCTV, so I had a lot of inspiration from those. And I come from skateboarding and sort of, that sort of … like, you mentioned *Being John Malkovich*—Spike Jonze came from skateboarding, and he's got that kind of out-of-the-box, punk rock attitude. So I think there's definitely a desire to, as you said, give the middle finger to the standard cookie-cutter movie, and probably a lot of those people I mentioned had the same kind of motivation when they made films. They were tired of seeing the same sort of predictable story and

> predictable style of shooting and predictable music and I definitely wanted to kind of change things up. Probably explains why I'm living in a van right now. I want to find new ways of doing things.[4]

Lynch, Cronenberg, and (arguably) Jonze are avant-garde filmmakers in the sense I have in mind. Their films transgress the conventions of mainstream filmmaking in ways that are widely considered to be cinematically exciting and artistically meritorious. As Green explains, his intention in making *Freddy Got Fingered* was also to defy the conventions of mainstream filmmaking. But then why is his film considered good-bad (or just bad, for many) while the films of Lynch and Cronenberg are received as highbrow avant-garde works? The main factor that determines how works are sorted between these categories is the *perception of artistic seriousness*. Lynch's *Mulholland Drive* and Cronenberg's *Videodrome* are seen as artistically serious works deserving of the attention of educated audiences, while *Freddy Got Fingered* has mostly been seen as a geek show for stoners and juveniles.

But the perception of artistic seriousness is often rooted in prejudice, fashion, and other ephemera (and the implicit binary misses an important demographic: educated stoners). Many works that are initially received as bad or good-bad end up getting assimilated into the received canon in retrospect. Frank Henenlotter's low-budget exploitation movie *Basket Case*, for instance, is now part of the permanent collection of the Museum of Modern Art. The Criterion Collection (widely perceived as a collection of movies that merit serious attention) now includes John Waters' *Polyester*, *Female Trouble*, and *Multiple Maniacs*, as well as a number of Godzilla sequels, such as *Ghidorah, the Three-Headed Monster* and *Invasion of Astro-Monster*. An internet search for revisionary takes on *Freddy Got Fingered* turns up a number of podcasts and essays heralding it as an avant-garde classic, and even a master's thesis claiming that it's a masterpiece of neo-Surrealism.[5]

The idea that there is an affinity between the good-bad and the avant-garde is supported by an empirical study conducted by Keyvan Sarkhosh and Winfried Menninghaus and analyzed in their 2016 article "Enjoying trash films: Underlying features, viewing stances, and experiential response dimensions." They conclude that fans of trash films like these films not just because they are fun and amusing, but also because they are transgressive of mainstream norms. Moreover, Sarkhosh and Menninghaus' findings suggest that trash film lovers are also likely to be interested in art cinema, which they also see as transgressive (the term "avant-garde" isn't used in the study, but this is a closely related category to art cinema).[6] The avant-garde and the good-bad are both characterized by the violation of received mainstream norms, but the avant-garde benefits from an aura of artistic seriousness (perhaps well-deserved, perhaps not), while the good-bad does not.

We arrive at an official definition:

> **Conventional badness:** violating received mainstream norms in a way that is not perceived as artistically serious.

There is widespread disagreement about which works are artistically serious and which ones are not, and so there is often corresponding disagreement about whether a work is properly considered avant-garde or simply bad. Stunningly, the first major book dedicated to bad movies (*The Fifty Worst Films of All Time*; Medved, Medved, and Dreyfuss 1978) lists Alain Resnais' *Last Year at Marienbad* as one of the worst movies ever made. Resnais' film is a crown jewel of cinematic modernism and more plausibly one of the *best* movies ever made. The authors call it "tedious" and "patently fraudulent," and cite numerous critics who dismiss it as pretentious and boring. This sort of backlash from critics against avant-garde art that they don't understand is extremely common. The charge of pretentiousness is used as a lazy bludgeon to substitute for insight. The rank absurdity of calling *Last Year at Marienbad* pretentious is a clear illustration of the way that perception of artistic seriousness tends to be arbitrary and fickle.

The term *film maudit* ("cursed film") was popularized by the 1949 *Festival du Film Maudit* in Biarritz, helmed by none other than poet and filmmaker Jean Cocteau, along with *Cahiers du Cinema* co-founder André Bazin. The festival celebrated films that the group of cinephiles who organized it believed were unfairly maligned or wrongly neglected, such as Jean Renoir's *The Southerner*, Jean Vigo's *L'Atalante* and *Zéro de conduite*, and John Ford's *The Long Voyage Home*. According to J. Hoberman in his 2021 essay "No success like failure – a natural history of the *film maudit*," Cocteau declared in the catalogue for the festival: "A great film is an accident, a banana skin under the feet of dogma," and the films to defend are "those that despise rules."[7] Most of the films that were screened at the festival went on to become canonical classics, but only through the persistent advocacy of people like Cocteau. This process has continued in a cyclical matter, with films ranging from Elaine May's *Ishtar* to Michael Cimino's *Heaven's Gate* bombing with critics and early audiences only to be rehabilitated through the efforts of ardent cinephiles who carry the torch of Cocteau's festival.

Hoberman defines a *film maudit* as one that is "widely panned even as it is staunchly defended by a devoted minority."[8]

Through most of film history, these devoted minorities have rarely had much of a platform, and so *film maudit* culture has largely remained in the margins. In the 21st century, however, the internet's democratization of mass communication has significantly changed film discourse and enabled communities built around outlier points of view to flourish.

Film scholar Peter Labuza writes:

> But the culture of *film maudit* has fundamentally changed with the emergence of a new cinephilia in the last decade. No longer are these films that were only seen by a handful of people decades ago, or stayed up late to watch on the Z Channel. Now the *film maudit* becomes the talk of Twitter, the film you must see because they (who "they" are is never specified) were unable to see the masterpiece hidden inside. Today such films are widely available, whether on director-approved Blu-rays or decidedly un-approved torrents made from digitized VHS tapes. The champions are no longer relegated to the outskirts—they are perhaps the center in many ways, all connected thanks to social media and able to form a community around their cinephiliac pleasures.[9]

Even as the popular face of the film industry has become increasingly homogenous, subcultures outside the Tomato consensus are thriving in the internet era. It's easy to find niche communities where neglected works like Cameron Crowe's *Aloha* and Lilly and Lana Wachowski's *Speed Racer* are prized. Depending on how one curates one's feed, it is entirely possible to live in a bubble in which everyone likes both Tony Scott's *Domino* (2005) *and* Brian De Palma's *Domino* (2019). From the point of view of someone like Labuza who is immersed in cinephile culture, the *film maudit* is no longer marginal at all—it is the center of attention.

But a thriving subculture is still a subculture, and even though the most of the people I follow on Twitter cherish George Lucas' *film maudit Attack of the Clones* and understand it in connection with his early work *THX 1138* and his background in experimental film, there is still a vast mainstream that haughtily mocks it and doesn't even imagine that it *might* be good. Lucas' prequel trilogy is still at an early stage of the process of reevaluation through which films see their reputations pass from critical rejection to cult fandom to highbrow canonization. Paul Verhoeven's *Showgirls* has gone through the complete cycle. It was initially received as a notorious turkey, then it became a cult hit that college students watched while playing *Showgirls*-themed drinking games, and before long it gained a reputation among highbrow commentators (including legendary New Wave director Jacques Rivette) as one of the greatest American films of the era.[10]

Good-bad film culture is a space where transgressive movies that are rejected by initial audiences can begin the process of reappraisal and rehabilitation. As Sarkhosh and Menninghaus's study indicates, there is a high degree of overlap between good-bad movie fans and art cinema fans. *Film maudit* culture emerges from this overlap. I don't mean to say that a legendary *film maudit* such as *Heaven's Gate* or *Showgirls* should be seen as good-bad. Rather, I mean that the *film maudit* sits at the nexus where the concepts of cinematic merit and artistic seriousness are problematized and reshaped. *Freddy Got Fingered* is a modern-day *film maudit*. It has a rating of 11% on the Tomatometer, but it is the frequent subject of essays with titles such as "15 Years Later, is 'Freddy Got Fingered' a Secret Masterpiece?"[11] Philosopher Elizabeth Cantalamessa has suggested that we should understand at least some aesthetic disagreement as *conceptual negotiation*, where we are not simply trying to *find out* whether or not an artwork has a given quality, but rather we are *advocating* for our own point of view about what it means to have this quality.[12]

The Guardian has a series called "Hear Me Out" in which writers "make the case for mostly hated films."[13] Each piece has a title in the form "Why X isn't a Bad Movie." Many of the movies discussed in the series are solidly in the *film maudit* category and have an established faction of devoted defenders (*Ishtar*, *Batman v Superman: Dawn of Justice*), others are good-bad cult favorites (*Speed 2: Cruise Control*, *The Island of Dr. Moreau*), and still others are widely thought of as simply bad and have very few defenders of any sort (*The Wedding Planner*, Roland Emmerich's *Godzilla*). These essays take a variety of approaches. Some of them argue that a movie in fact succeeds according to conventional standards when most critics think it fails. Others grant that a movie fails to meet a certain set of standards but argue that it is nevertheless fun to watch or valuable in some other way. My favorite is Steve Rose's piece on Guy Ritchie's *King Arthur: Legend of the Sword*, in which he vigorously defends Ritchie's stylistic panache and presents a compelling interpretation of the film as a commentary on British identity. Most of the essays in the series are quite measured, but they are interesting insofar as they are perfect examples of people trying to come to terms with aesthetic concepts and apply them in unorthodox ways. There's no way that anyone is defending Roland Emmerich's *Godzilla* without engaging in a bit of the ol' conceptual negotiation. In his piece on that film, Edward Tew writes: "Mindless isn't always an insult."[14] Tew agrees with the common charge that the film is mindless, but argues that mindlessness isn't an inherently negative quality.

When we argue about whether a movie such as *Freddy Got Fingered* is good, bad, or good-bad, we are arguing in part about what it means to be good or bad (or serious or unserious) and what criteria we should be using. Suppose you think that *Freddy Got Fingered* is a good-bad movie and I'm trying to convince you that it's simply good. I might argue thus: "*Freddy Got Fingered* is not so bad it's good, it's an avant-garde provocation. It's the height of postmodernism, and the fact that no one realized this at the time is just more evidence that it *is* the height of postmodernism." This argument does not propose that the film is good according to the same criteria that others are using when they judge that it's bad. Rather, this argument proposes that others have been looking at it the wrong way and using the wrong criteria. If you're not convinced, you might retort that the level of juvenilia *Freddy* displays excludes it from being considered a serious work of art, and therefore that it should be considered good-bad rather than good. I might respond that this is prejudice and there is no inherent limit to the level of juvenilia that the concept of artistic seriousness can accommodate. I could point to Harmony Korine's *Trash Humpers* as a movie that's at least as juvenile but has gotten a more sympathetic reception, no doubt because Korine has a reputation as a serious artist while Tom Green does not. As this dialectic develops, we are not just arguing about *Freddy Got Fingered*, we are arguing about the concept of "artistic seriousness" and the criteria we use to apply it.

***

Let's return to the distinction I introduced earlier between Bad Movie Love and Bad Movie Ridicule:

> **Love:** Appreciating a movie in virtue of the ways in which it violates conventional norms and sincerely and directly enjoying it.

Ridicule: Mocking a movie in virtue of the ways in which it violates conventional norms, relishing schadenfreude at the expense of the artists who made the movie, and/or enjoying jokes made at the movie's expense.

Ridicule is a more contemptuous way of engaging with bad movies, where the point is not to appreciate them, but rather to have fun at their expense. Practitioners of Ridicule say things such as: "This movie is a piece of garbage, but it's unintentionally funny." They gather in groups to mock bad movies out loud while watching them, in the style of *Mystery Science Theater* 3000 or its descendant *RiffTrax*. There is an ever-expanding glut of podcasts and YouTube channels that walk this path. When people engage with bad movies in this way, the experience they are after involves some combination of disdain, schadenfreude, and amusement at their own jokes about the movie. One of my overall aims in this book is to make a plea for engaging with bad movies in the mode of Love instead of Ridicule. Bad Movie Love fosters creative forms of engagement that break out of restrictive mainstream norms. Ridicule affirms and reinforces these norms by disparaging movies that violate them.

When practitioners of Ridicule say that a movie is "so bad it's good," they mean that it is bad in both the conventional sense and the final sense, but that they still enjoy watching it because of the schadenfreude and mockery it enables. When Bad Movie Lovers say that a movie is "so bad it's good," in contrast, they mean that a movie is good in the final sense partly in virtue of being bad in the conventional sense. They are saying that the movie is worth engaging with in part because of the ways that it violates mainstream norms, but they are also acknowledging that it doesn't (yet) have the aura of artistic seriousness that would qualify it for the avant-garde. There is certainly some cultural overlap between Love and Ridicule, and many people enjoy both ways of interacting with bad movies, but they are distinct practices.

One might object at this stage that I am oversimplifying the attitudes that Bad Movie Lovers have towards bad movies. It might appear that there is *some* sense in which they find bad movies aesthetically disvaluable. Even the most committed Bad Movie Lover sometimes cringes at unnatural dialogue or winces at particularly messy editing while enjoying a bad movie. Does this show that their response to the movie is at least partially negative? I don't think so. It's very common for negative emotions to function positively in the context of art appreciation. When horror movies disgust us, tragedies make us feel intense pity, or comedies make us cringe with vicarious embarrassment, that's often a good thing. Something similar is true for bad movies: cringing and wincing can be part of the fun. If I cringe at John Travolta's performance in the 2019 film *The Fanatic*, this can add to my enjoyment in much the same was that cringing adds to my enjoyment when Jason Biggs' character gets caught having sex with a pie in *American Pie*. Both are painfully funny.

***

It still remains to explain *why* we like the sort of transgression we find in good-bad movies. Much of this book will be spent exploring a wide variety of good-bad movies and the many reasons people love them, but our discussion so far points to some initial thoughts. Speaking for myself, multiple decades and many thousands of movies into my personal journey as a cinephile, I've reached a stage where I find most critically acclaimed prestige movies bland and dull. A ridiculous accent or the sudden appearance of an unexplained boat can really liven things up. I find joy and fulfillment in the exploratory process of developing idiosyncratic ways of thinking about movies. If I spent as much of my life engaging with the art form as I have and came out of it without a distinctive point of view, that wouldn't be a very good sign as to the quality of my project. It took a lot of work to have such terrible opinions. But—again—the magic of the internet is that I'm not alone. Although most of the people I know from ordinary contexts have very different taste in movies than I do, there are *multitudes* of online communities where I can interact with like-minded movie lovers. Such communities provide a context for the cultivation of unorthodox views, but also function to limit how far into the wilderness it's fruitful to go in our bad movie explorations. I might come up with an exotic interpretation of Roland Emmerich's *Godzilla* where it starts to look interesting, but if my interpretation doesn't have adequate grounding in the movie itself, I won't have much success reaping the values of community engagement when I initiate discussions about it. If I propose, for example, that Emmerich is a crypto-Maoist, this is probably a path that I will have to walk on my own.

I've suggested that movies are good in the final sense if they are worthy of our time and attention. To return to that thought, my big theory (which I will develop further in Chapter 6) is that, in general, the aesthetic value of an artwork or other aesthetic object consists in its capacity to support valuable activities of engagement. By "activity of engagement," I mean an activity of engaging with an artwork as such in the mode of appreciation. Using a novel as a Frisbee is not a way of engaging with it *as an artwork* and so is not an activity of engagement. Mocking a movie and cracking jokes while it plays might be a way of engaging with it as an artwork, but not in the mode of appreciation, and so it also does not count as an activity of engagement in my sense. Appreciation necessarily involves taking a positive stance towards a work.

Activities of engagement are valuable when they make our lives better. I've already suggested two ways in which bad movies have enabled valuable activities of engagement for me. First, they've given me a path to deepen my cinephilia. It wouldn't be very interesting to spend a large portion of my life engaging with movies in the precise ways that are prescribed by received mainstream norms. There's not much room for creativity or self-expression along that path. My love of bad movies has given me a space to carve out my own way of seeing things (and here I am, writing a book about it). Second, bad movies have served as a basis for a variety of social relationships, including personal friendships as well as participation in larger communities. These social relationships are grounded in shared appreciation of good-bad movies.

So then, what would it take for a Bad Movie Lover to judge a movie to be bad in the *final* sense? On my theory, a movie is bad in the final sense if it is unable to support valuable activities of engagement. I gave the example earlier of the 2019 film *Head Count*. If the director of *Head Count* happens to read this, I apologize for picking on your movie in particular. I just happened to watch it right before I started writing this book. In any case, the reason I consider *Head Count* to be bad in the final sense is that there's just nothing there to sink your teeth into. In the case of *The Core*, if I try to watch it in the mode of hard sci-fi, it doesn't have much to offer. But if I look at it as a campy retro spectacle, I start to find fruitful pathways of engagement. With *Head Count*, no matter how many different ways I try to look at the movie, it just won't give up the goods. Could I be missing something? Maybe! And that's part of the value of bad movie communities. Someone else might find something in *Head Count* that I didn't find, and they might even convince me to give it another chance and try looking at it in the way they suggest. For now, however, when I try to engage with the film, I come up empty handed, and so my judgment is that it's bad in the final sense.

***

Susan Sontag was one of the first authors to write about Bad Movie Love. In her influential 1964 piece "Notes on 'Camp'," she wrote about movies as part of her more general portrait of camp.[15] Camp has its origins in gay subculture and has long revered over-the-top movie stars including Bette Davis and Joan Crawford, who have been lovingly emulated in drag performances for decades.[16] Sontag's piece is a helpful starting point as we consider what there is to love about bad movies and why Bad Movie Love is a superior form of engagement to Ridicule.

"Notes on 'Camp'" is made up of a series of epigrams that characterize the camp sensibility. Here are several that are especially relevant to the topic of good-bad movies:

> 23. In naïve, or pure, Camp, the essential element is seriousness, a seriousness that fails. Of course, not all seriousness that fails can be redeemed as Camp. Only that which has the proper mixture of the exaggerated, the fantastic, the passionate, and the naïve.
> 24. When something is just bad (rather than Camp), it's often because it is too mediocre in its ambition. The artist hasn't attempted to do anything really outlandish. ("It's too

much," "It's too fantastic," "It's not to be believed," are standard phrases of Camp enthusiasm.)

25. The hallmark of Camp is the spirit of extravagance. Camp is a woman walking around in a dress made of three million feathers. Camp is the paintings of Carlo Crivelli, with their real jewels and trompe-l'oeil insects and cracks in the masonry. Camp is the outrageous aestheticism of Steinberg's six American movies with Dietrich, all six, but especially the last, *The Devil Is a Woman*.

34. Camp taste turns its back on the good-bad axis of ordinary aesthetic judgment. Camp doesn't reverse things. It doesn't argue that the good is bad, or the bad is good. What it does is to offer for art (and life) a different—a supplementary—set of standards.

Camp, on Sontag's account, does not merely swap the bad for the good—some bad art is just bland and forgettable—but rather adopts an alternative set of standards. This alternative set of standards values failed seriousness that "has the proper mixture of the exaggerated, the fantastic, the passionate, and the naïve." She offers the example of a woman walking around in a dress made of three million feathers. There's a seriousness to this fashion statement; a dress made of three million feathers is expensive and requires a lot of highly skilled labor to construct. It's not a look that one throws together on a lark. Walking around in a dress made of three million feathers is a deliberate expression of style. It's passionate and naïve: the person who invested in this dress truly means it. But it's also fantastic and exaggerated to the point of absurdity. The risk of looking like Big Bird is right there lying in wait. One can't wear a dress made of three million feathers and not resemble Big Bird to at least some extent. The ridiculousness of the look, the serious effort it took to achieve, and the swagger with which it is worn together create the effect of being *too much*, and that is exactly what the camp sensibility admires about it. Wearing a dress made of three million feathers displays a spirit of extravagance that can be admired in a way that a classically elegant fashion statement cannot.

The six Josef von Sternberg movies that Sontag mentions all showcase Marlene Dietrich's singular persona. When she slinks onscreen in some extravagant outfit, she gives the impression of not being of this world. She's impossibly sexy. Everything about her defies restrictive norms of female modesty. In *Shanghai Express*, she plays an infamous courtesan named Shanghai Lily. When she meets a former lover aboard the titular train, she explains that she's changed her name since their time together. "Married?" he asks. "It took more than one man to change my name to Shanghai Lily." This line sends a tingle down my spine—has any character ever cared less what anyone thinks of them? The realization dawns on him: "So *you're* Shanghai Lily … ." Unashamed, she confirms: "The notorious white flower of China. You heard of me, and you always believed what you heard."

By no account are the Sternberg/Dietrich collaborations bad movies, but they exhibit what Sontag calls "outrageous aestheticism." In the 1930s, when these films were made, the influence of the silent era was still running strong. Lacking spoken dialogue, silent movies often relied on visual exaggeration to make their content legible. The Sternberg/Dietrich movies emerged from the deliciously strange transitional phase when the exaggerations of the silent era carried over into sound films. Although several of the Sternberg/Dietrich movies are dramas with heavy themes, their dramatic weight is entangled with their fundamental outrageousness.

A common theme in Sternberg is the dignity of dying on one's own terms. Characters in his movies—including some played by Dietrich—respond to certain doom by greeting it with an assertion of agency and self-possession. The seriousness of this theme doesn't conflict with the movies' exaggerated aestheticism, but rather amplifies it. Sternberg's shadowy, expressionistic compositions and Dietrich's persona are natural extensions of the films' fatalistic subject matter. Her brash indifference towards the norms of polite society extends all the way to her attitude towards death. There's a moment in *Dishonored* when she freshens her lipstick just before facing a firing squad (image 3). It's the single most badass thing anyone's ever done in a movie.

Image 3: *Dishonored* (1931) (Credit: Paramount Studios)

Unfortunately, Sontag oversimplifies things when she analyzes camp as characteristically involving *failed seriousness*. In addition to being a poor fit for many of her own examples, including the Sternberg films (which don't fail at anything), this phrase risks giving the impression that camp enjoyment involves disdain for its object. Indeed, despite how strenuously I'm insisting that Bad Movie Love is a different practice from Ridicule, this is a risk that my own account faces: if one loves a movie *because it's bad*, doesn't that necessarily involve some measure of mockery and disdain? I hope not! I will take up this issue more fully in Chapter 4, but Sontag gives us a helpful starting point. She writes:

> 55. Camp taste is, above all, a mode of enjoyment, of appreciation—not judgment. Camp is generous. It wants to enjoy. It only seems like malice, cynicism. (Or, if it is cynicism, it's not a ruthless but a sweet cynicism.) Camp taste doesn't propose that it is in bad taste to be serious; it doesn't sneer at someone who succeeds in being seriously dramatic. What it does is to find the success in certain passionate failures.
> 56. Camp taste is a kind of love, love for human nature. It relishes, rather than judges, the little triumphs and awkward intensities of "character."... Camp taste identifies with what it is enjoying. People who share this sensibility are not laughing at the thing they label as "a camp," they're enjoying it. Camp is a tender feeling.

Sontag thinks that camp sensibility relishes failed seriousness, but not in the mode of disdain. It doesn't mock its object for its intended seriousness or for having failed to achieve it.

Rather, camp sensibility *admires* the eccentricity of character revealed by an extravagant failure.

Contrast two attitudes towards a woman wearing a dress made of three million feathers:

Ridicule: Check out Ms. Big Bird over there. Doesn't she just look awful? What a waste of money that awful dress must have been.

Camp: That dress is just too much! It's fantastic. Oh, my, what a bold spirt must lie behind those feathers.

As Sontag puts it, camp *finds the success* in a certain type of failed seriousness. A dress made of three million feathers may not succeed in the straightforward way that less extravagant sartorial choices sometimes do, but it *does* succeed as an expression of an eccentric sensibility. Sneering at a woman in a dress made of three million feathers reveals an unenviable aesthetic smallness. Camp is grand and generous.

Contrast two different reactions to *The Core*:

Rotten Tomatoes user Julie T.: "If we are taking this seriously, and as there are no particular nods to this being a parody, this is possibly the most inane disaster movie ever, not saved at all by a pretty strong cast who were obviously only there to try and give an impression that you were going to see a quality product, trust me your not. The plot is so ridiculous that an out and out parady would have been the way to go, but no the producers here try and sell us a movie so ludicrous an infants school pupil would be able to knock holes in the sudo science presented. Steer incredibly well clear, unless watching the most idiotic distaster movie of all time is your thing, in which case sit back and enjoy." [sic.]

Rotten Tomatoes user Mvke S.: "Really good. Great cast. I want to go to the core."

Julie T. (and the majority of other Rotten Tomatoes users who have posted reviews of the film) balk at the tension between the absurdity and seriousness of *The Core*. They complain that the premise is unrealistic and the science is inaccurate. Julie T. is explicitly unhappy about the lack of signaling that the movie is *intentionally* ridiculous. If it were a clear parody, the fake science would be more acceptable to her.

By logging on to Rotten Tomatoes and panning the film in this manner, Julie T. and others are doing their small part to enforce received norms and punish the movie for violating them. It's like sneering at a woman in a dress made of three million feathers. Their contempt reveals an impoverished imagination and regretable narrowness. This is not to say that everyone ought to enjoy *The Core*, but rather that adopting such a haughty, derisive tone towards such a ridiculous movie is deeply unimpressive. I'm far more excited by Mvke S.'s take: *I want to go to the core.*

***

Susan Sontag's portrait of camp sensibility takes us to the fiery molten core of Bad Movie Love. Camp adopts a *loving, tender* attitude towards its objects. Making a movie involves a lot of work and personal sacrifice from the team behind it. When the result of all this work and sacrifice is an earnest hot mess, we are given an opportunity to relish human eccentricity in all its glory. I suspect the scale of film production is a big part of why good-bad movies have taken off in a way that good-bad watercolor painting never has. In a world full of reckless ambition, it should be immensely gratifying to see so much effort deployed so absurdly. Think about what it took to make *The Core*! What a grand monument to the ridiculousness of the human condition! To treat such a beautiful oddity as a mere opportunity for mockery and derision is at best a failure of imagination: "Hey you tried really hard to make a movie and it turned out not to fit my notions of what a movie should be like. Let's have a laugh at all the ways you've failed!" It's not a nice attitude, and not an attitude I would enjoy adopting.

One of my primary aims over the remainder of this book is to make the case that Bad Movie Love is the better path. Ridiculing bad movies involves holding them to conventional standards and enjoying their failure to meet these standards. While conventional standards have a positive role to play in our aesthetic lives, narrow adherence to them is a quick route to a stagnant film culture. Bad Movie Love is a way of rebelling against aesthetic homogenization, and I submit that such rebellion is badly needed. There has been a strong tendency towards homogenization in mainstream cinema in recent years. Just look at the ascendency of the Disney empire.

In 2017, Disney had a 21.8% market share of American box office earnings. In 2018, this was up to 26%. In 2019, it was up to 33.1%.[17] I'm not here to debate the merit of Disney's films, but regardless of one's stance on them, I hope we can all agree that such pronounced market dominance is bad for cinema. Disney finds something that people like and then they do it over and over and over again. We've all noticed that the multiplex is more saturated than ever with sequels and franchise titles. Disney is well-known to exert creative control over its productions to ensure a high degree of aesthetic continuity within a franchise. Edgar Wright quit the production of *Ant-Man* because he became convinced that Disney wouldn't let him make a movie reflecting his own creative sensibility.[18]

Similarly, Chris Lord and Phil Miller were fired from *Solo* in part because their approach was too distinctive and would have stood apart too strongly from the rest of the *Star Wars* series.[19]

The Rotten Tomatoes aggregate is another homogenizing force. The Tomatometer creates the ridiculous impression that questions of aesthetic value should be decided by majority rule. This is a fundamentally flawed approach, because we should expect that many of the most interesting artworks will be subject to intense disagreement, especially when they are first released. Anything that's genuinely bold and risky is going to turn some people off. Even Alfred Hitchcock's *Vertigo*, now widely considered one of the greatest films of all time, was poorly received when it was initially released in 1958. *New Yorker* critic John McCarten wrote: "Alfred Hitchcock, who produced and directed this thing, has never before indulged in such farfetched nonsense."[20] The film didn't gain its hallowed reputation until the late 1970s and early 80s, after it was removed from circulation for ten years and then rereleased.

There are many ways to oppose the trend of homogenization, and Bad Movie Love is one of them. I don't put much trust in the Tomatometer, but if there's a movie with John Travolta in it that has a score below 25%, I'm definitely in. The aggregate tends to track the extent to which a movie adheres to received norms and standards. The mainstream publications that employ most Top Tomato Critics don't want to hire someone who loves *Freddy Got Fingered* and *The Core* but dislikes *Toy Story 4* and *Avengers: Endgame*. They want someone who agrees with the pack most of the time. Genuine outliers, such as Armond White, have often been the subject of widespread condemnation, angry petitions, and even outright harassment for defying the Tomato Consensus. Fans are perennially enraged when a critic with a distinctive outlook "ruins" the perfect score of some trendy new movie they want to think of as officially sanctioned. The Tomatometer and its enforcers surely have a chilling effect on critical dissent. No one wants to be the critic who didn't like the talking toy movie and as a result gets harassed and singled out by a petition demanding they be removed from the aggregate and fired from their job. In this way, Rotten Tomatoes creates a feedback loop that supports the dominance of convention and rewards homogeneity. Good-bad movies, as I have characterized them, are, by definition, movies that resist convention (deliberately or not). Appreciative engagement with such movies is a way of resisting the groupthink of the critical mainstream.

Craig Brewer's 2019 film *Dolemite Is My Name* portrays this dynamic beautifully. Rudy Ray Moore (played by Eddie Murphy) and his ragtag crew of misfits make a totally absurd movie full of inept kung fu and gratuitous nudity and they have an absolute blast doing it. All the studio executives can see when they look at it is its shoddy production value, but audiences respond much differently. They laugh heartily—not with disdain, but with love and appreciation. Moore and his crew weren't trying to make a comedy, but they welcome the audience's laughter as a celebration of their vision. *Dolemite Is My Name* conveys the joy of making and watching movies without regard for the stifling received norms that the studio executives are portrayed as being in the grip of.

There is, however, a pitfall that we must be wary of. In his influential 2002 essay, "Cult fictions: Cult Movies, subcultural capital and the production of cultural distinctions," scholar Mark Jancovich makes the entirely fair point that cult movie fans self-servingly construct "mainstream film culture" as an inauthentic monolith that dominates the taste of unwary dupes. This sort of countercultural snobbery is obnoxious.

I don't want to be that guy and I don't want to write that book. I have no problem with the mainstream as such; my problem is with its tendency to crowd other things out. I'm not here to indict the mainstream; I'm here to defend films that stand outside of it and make a case for open-mindedness and the celebration of diverse sensibilities.

***

Here's the plan:

In Chapter 2, we'll take a close look at what's so great about three of the worst movies ever made, and consider the question of whether we're doing something wrong when we watch a movie in a different way than the filmmaker intended. In Chapter 3, we'll zoom out to get a broader view of the different types of good-bad movies that are out there and the different ways they can be appreciated. In Chapter 4, we'll consider the concept of taste through the lens of my personal journey with the *Twilight* movies. In Chapter 5, we'll explore the acting career of Nicolas Cage, examining the way in which mainstream norms and popular perceptions tend to limit the critical imagination and block appreciation of bold and ambitious artistry. Finally, in Chapter 6, we'll consider whether bad movies deserve a place in the good life or whether we'd be better off without them.

Artists' Intentions and Bad Movie Greatness

Two

In this chapter, we'll consider three movies that are often cited as being among the best-worst movies of all time: *Plan 9 from Outer Space*, *Troll 2*, and *The Room*.

One thing these movies have in common is that there is a divide between the way their creators intended them and the way audiences have engaged with them. This raises a difficult question: is there anything wrong with appreciating a movie in a different way than the artists who made it intended?

***

In 1978, Michael and Harry Medved along with Randy Dreyfuss popularized the practice of ranking bad movies with their book *The Fifty Worst Films of All Time*. The prize for first place went to Ed Wood's *Plan 9 from Outer Space*, cementing its place in the bad movie pantheon. It's a low-budget sci-fi B movie, bankrolled by Baptist ministers. Notably, it's the final film of horror icon Bela Lugosi, who died during production.

Plan 9's bad movie qualifications are considerable. The premise alone would be sufficient: an alien species is concerned that humanity will destroy the entire universe by developing a bomb that will detonate the sun, and so they have come to Earth to warn the American government, but they've been ignored. So, to get our attention, they use a ray gun to resurrect

DOI: 10.4324/9780367808969-2

several corpses in a small town. The question of why the aliens choose a small town instead of Washington D.C., or some other metropolis, is never addressed.

The dialogue and narration feel as though they were written by someone with very limited experience of the way human beings actually talk. The very first line of the narration is: "Greetings, my friend. We are all interested in the future, for that is where you and I are going to spend the rest of our lives. And remember, my friend, future events such as these will affect you in the future."

The film is full of continuity lapses and obtrusive failures to sustain the pretenses of the fiction. We see the police leave for the graveyard in daylight and arrive at night in a different car. Once they arrive, one of the cops casually uses his gun to adjust his hat and then rests the gun on his chest, pointing at his face, with his finger on the trigger (image 4). The tombstones are

Image 4: Plan 9 from Outer Space (1957) (Credit: Reynolds Pictures, Inc.)

made of thin cardboard and they wobble when the actors bump into them. The "death ray" is a flashlight. Extras smile at the camera. The editing is … nonstandard. The music is sometimes cut off in the middle of a phrase, stock footage is roughly integrated, and after Lugosi died during filming Wood chose to just reuse a shot of him walking across a cemetery multiple times.

There are plenty of shoddily made movies out there. What makes *Plan 9* stand out is that its bizarre dialogue, transparently artificial production design, nonsensical narrative, thematic wonkiness, jagged editing, and disregard for continuity come together in a way that almost feels like a unified vision—like someone might have made it this way on purpose as an avant-garde experiment. J. Hoberman famously connected Ed Wood with the avant-garde in his 1980 *Film Comment* piece, "Bad movies":

> For Walter Benjamin (and even André Bazin), the seamless "equipment-free aspect of reality" that movies presented on screen was actually the "height of artifice." The objectively bad film acknowledges this: the lie of "chronology" is confounded by imperfect continuity; "invisible" editing is ruptured by mismatched cuts; mise-en-scène is foregrounded by cloddish bits of business. A good bad movie is a philosophers' stone that converts the incompetent mistakes of naïve dross into modernist gold. Such movies are unstable objects. They ping-pong back and forth from diegetic intent to profilmic event (or to their own jerry-built construction) the way a Cezanne oscillates between a representational landscape and a paint-gopped canvas.[1]

One of the hallmarks of modernism and the avant-garde, both in film and other media, is drawing attention to the artificiality of representational means. A painting by Cezanne may represent a landscape, but the techniques he used in crafting this representation foreground the fact that one is looking at gops of paint on a canvas. All paintings of trees consist in gops of paint on a canvas rather than actual trees, but realist paintings create a sense of illusion while a Cezanne prompts us to see the paint as paint. If one spends some time looking at a Cezanne landscape, one will likely fluctuate back and forth between focusing on the gops of paint as such and the emergent representational image.

The equivalent in cinema are films that make us aware of the means of their production and shatter the illusions that they themselves create. Ingmar Bergman's *Persona* is a classic example. Late in the movie, the film itself appears to rip, disrupting the illusory reality we had been immersed in and making us aware that we are watching a film. Other famous examples include Alejandro Jodorowsky's *The Holy Mountain* and Abbas Kiarostami's *Taste of Cherry*, which both end by showing us the production crew responsible for the very film we've been watching.

These films deliberately highlight their own artifice. *Plan 9 from Outer Space* does so without trying. What we initially see as a tombstone is revealed as a cardboard prop when someone bumps into it. Two flying saucers and a planet they fly around are revealed as miniatures when we see the shadow of one of the saucers pass over the planet. *Plan 9* mirrors the avant-garde by violating the codes of Hollywood filmmaking. The film's lapses of continuity resemble deliberate surrealism. Wood's repeated use of the shot of Lugosi walking across the graveyard could have been a modernist editing decision. Hoberman's suggestion is that the film becomes more interesting if we look at it in this way, and nothing stops us from doing so.

Hoberman's take on *Plan 9* has become an important example for philosophers of art concerned with the question of how we should take an artist's intentions into account when engaging with their work. Philosopher Noël Carroll argues that engaging with a work of art is akin to having a conversation with the artist.[2] In a conversation, we seek to interpret the other person's utterances in light of what we think they are intended to convey. If we refuse to do this and attribute meanings to these utterances that conflict with what we have reason to believe they are intended to express, then (other things being equal) we are being bad conversationalists. Similarly, Carroll thinks, when engaging with art, if we ignore the artist's intentions and interpret their work however we like, we are being a bad audience. For a great work of art, this can mean missing out on a great conversation. But he thinks we also have reason to restrict our interpretation according to our beliefs about the artist's intentions for bad works of art. In the case of Ed Wood, he frames this as a matter of self-respect. He argues that while the avant-garde is interested in transgressing the codes of Hollywood filmmaking, Ed Wood attempted to adhere to these codes but did a terrible job of it. Although it might be more engaging for the audience to think of *Plan 9* in terms of the avant-garde, Carroll thinks that it is more important to sustain our conversational integrity, where we limit our ways of seeing artworks according to what we think their creator might have intended. He writes:

> Aesthetic arguments for anti-intentionalism proceed as if aesthetic satisfaction were the only important interest we could have with respect to artworks. Thus, wherever other putative interests impede aesthetic interests, they must give way. But aesthetic satisfaction is not the only major

> source of value that we have in interacting with artworks; the interaction is also a matter of a conversation between the artist and us—a human encounter—in which we have a desire to know what the artist intends, not only out of respect for the artist, but also because we have a personal interest in being a capable respondent. In endorsing the anti-intentionalist view that aesthetic satisfaction trumps all other interests, we seem to be willing to go for aesthetic pleasure at all costs, including, most notably, any value we might place on having a genuine conversational exchange with another human being. For, as the *Plan 9* example suggests, we are willing to act as if we had encountered a profound, reflexive meditation on the dominant cinema, when, in fact, it is readily apparent that we are dealing with a botched and virtually incoherent atrocity.[3]

Here and elsewhere, Carroll speaks of *Plan 9* with disdain: it's a botched atrocity, a schlock quicky, a failure to imitate the Hollywood style, a collection of mistakes from an incompetent director with insufficient funding. He presents these evaluations as the inevitable conclusions that someone earnestly engaged in conversation with Ed Wood's film would draw, while he presents Hoberman's take as an example of interpretive gerrymandering, where one tries to find whatever interpretation will give one the most aesthetic satisfaction.

Carroll presents us with a false dilemma; he has an unduly narrow idea of what an appropriate conversational posture looks like. Suppose I am taking an evening stroll and I bump into a man dressed in a purple tuxedo—complete with a purple top hat—who wants to talk about aerospace engineering. He clearly does not know anything about aerospace engineering, but that doesn't stop him from volunteering his theory that a spaceship shaped like a duck would be far more effective than traditional rocket designs. He entreats me to join him at the duck pond for further discussion. At this point, I could adopt the sort of severe and judgmental tone that Carroll takes towards Ed Wood:

> My good sir! Don't you think the esteemed employees of NASA would have shaped a ship like a duck if indeed a duck shape were advantageous? Do you mean to impugn the intelligence of these fine people? What qualifications do you possess that situate you to reach conclusions that are unavailable to them? None, I would think! I say good day to you, sir. I shall not accompany you to the duck pond to hear any further insinuations towards the good people at NASA.

But isn't there another posture available that may in fact be more appropriate? Couldn't I join him at the duck pond and play along with the conversation in order to enjoy and admire his display of eccentricity? To be clear, I don't mean that it might be amusing to play along in order to make fun of him. That would be cruel. It is possible to appreciate this sort of eccentric display without implying an insult. If he were to ask me bluntly what I think of his ideas, I would proffer a fist bump and respond: "I'm not convinced by your theory, but I like your style and I admire your imagination and creativity, my purple dude." This is an honest and open response that should not besmirch the dignity of our tuxedoed companion.

Isn't the same conversational posture available for Ed Wood? Carroll is wrong to characterize Wood as nothing more than an incompetent director trying and failing to imitate the Hollywood style. Wood was a movie fanatic as a kid and a lifelong fan of horror icons such as Lugosi. His Hollywood aspirations were born of his love for film. He befriended the elderly Lugosi, neglected by Hollywood and beset with morphine addiction, and put him in movies when no one else wanted to. As someone without skill or experience, it wasn't easy to convince anyone to fund his projects, but he remained doggedly persistent and when he came up short he went ahead and made movies anyways with what little resources he could scrape together. For Wood, making movies was the consummation of a lifelong passion.

Plan 9 wasn't his first film. He previously made a few others, including the remarkable 1953 feature *Glen or Glenda*. Wood was a crossdresser, and he made the film (which features Lugosi as a doctor who talks like Count Dracula) in part as a plea for tolerance of gender nonconformity. The movie lacks today's vocabulary for talking about gender and there are moments that haven't aged well, but, in other respects, it is surprisingly acute. It clarifies, for instance, the distinction between being a crossdresser and being transgender. It also clarifies that crossdressing is independent from homosexuality and that many men who like to dress in women's clothes also prefer women as sexual partners. It presents a robust defense of gender nonconformity, comparing bigotry against crossdressers to early opposition to automobiles and airplanes. Wood compares the statements "if God wanted us to fly, he would have given us wings" and "if God wanted us to roll around the countryside, he would have given us wheels" to the statement "if God wanted him to dress as a woman, he would have made him a woman."

Glen or Glenda has many of the same bad movie traits that *Plan 9* does, but it also makes clear that filmmaking for Ed Wood was about more than just cheaply slapping together an imitation of the Hollywood style. Wood appears in the film as the titular crossdresser Glen(da), and there is no question that the movie is very personal for him. There's a wild dream sequence featuring Satan and S&M imagery that is deliberately surreal. It's a movie from a director whose artistic ambition outstripped his funding and ability.

How one takes *Plan 9* should not simply be a matter of whether one sees its distinctive features as deliberate transgressions or inadvertent mistakes. Even if the movie is full of mistakes, we can still ask what *these particular mistakes* reveal about Wood's artistic sensibility. To put it simply, his sensibility is absurd. Using the shot of Lugosi crossing the cemetery over and over again was an absurd idea. The dialogue is absurd. The production design is absurd. The editing is absurd. It's an absurd movie, and it reveals its director's absurd point of view. Sure, *Plan 9* includes a lot of plain mistakes that Wood would have probably preferred to avoid, but the very fact that his work is so riddled with such mistakes reveals something about his approach as an artist. He was not in any way inspired towards caution by his inexperience and limited means. He went for it: flying saucers, ray guns, corpses rising from the dead. No money for props? Make 'em cheap! Cardboard tombstones it is. No money for that shot? Stock footage! Wood's sensibility is not just manifested by what he did deliberately, it's also manifested by the brazen manner in which he made his mistakes. Carroll argues that because Wood did not *intend* to transgress, the movie's oddities should not be seen as transgressions. But Ed Wood's point of view and approach to making movies was *already* transgressive, he didn't need to *try* to transgress.

We can admire Ed Wood, and we can admire him sincerely, without mockery or ridicule. Tim Burton clearly does: his biopic *Ed Wood* reflects a warm, loving attitude towards Wood and his films. When engaging with *Plan 9*, it is a perfectly appropriate conversational posture to admire the sensibility the film manifests while recognizing that it fails in various ways to realize the aims Wood had in making it. Just as I can admire the eccentricity of our duck-loving friend in the purple tuxedo, I can admire the sincere absurdity of Ed Wood.

One of Noël Carroll's arguments against appreciating *Plan 9* in the way that Hoberman suggests is that there's something perverse about interpreting art not as it was intended, but in the way that would maximize aesthetic satisfaction. Carroll has a point. It would indeed be perverse if we went around trying to find the way of interpreting every artwork we encounter where it turns out the most aesthetically satisfying. Some people might find it more aesthetically satisfying, for example, to think of *Gone with the Wind* as an elaborate satire of old Hollywood's racist archetypes and romantic view of the Confederacy, or to interpret Roland Emmerich's *Godzilla* as a Maoist parable.

If we were to go around interpreting every work of art in the way that gives us the most aesthetic satisfaction, we would leave behind an important element of art appreciation: discriminating artistic achievement. If someone is interested in the medium of film, it's important to be able to understand why *Citizen Kane* is an incredible artistic achievement while *The Sex Lives of the Potato Men* is not. If we treat every work as a great achievement just waiting to be seen in the right light, then we unduly lower *Citizen Kane* and elevate *The Sex Lives of the Potato Men*. In developing our ability to evaluate art, it's just as important to judge failure as success.

But appreciating *Plan 9 from Outer Space* in the way I've described is *not* simply a matter of maximizing aesthetic satisfaction. When we celebrate the absurdity of Wood's point of view, we celebrate qualities that the movie really does have. And we can celebrate these qualities without considering the movie to be a great artistic achievement. Ed Wood is not Orson Welles, *Plan 9* is not *Citizen Kane*, and that's okay. *Plan 9* has something different to offer. It's not the tremendous display of skill and vision that *Citizen Kane* is, but, as I will argue in Chapter 6, our engagement with art shouldn't just consist in seeking out the greatest artistic achievements all the time. There is room in a balanced cinematic diet to cherish both the finest masterworks and the most outrageous displays of eccentricity.

***

For most of the latter half of the 20th century, Italy was the epicenter of the great tradition of European exploitation movies. Exploitation movies are movies that seek to turn a profit by keeping production costs low and attracting an audience through the exploitation of marketable content, especially sex and violence. By 1990, the best days of Italian exploitation had passed, but a number of stalwarts kept pumping out wild movies on the cheap. Perhaps the most notorious title to come out of that late era was Claudio Fragasso's *Troll 2*. Mind-bogglingly bizarre in both concept and execution, it has justly become a cult favorite and is widely considered one of the greatest bad movies of all time.

Troll 2 is a useful case in part because we have a clear record of the cast and crew's attitude towards its reception. Michael Stephenson, who appeared in the film as a child actor, directed the 2009 documentary *Best Worst Movie* about *Troll 2* and its cult of fandom. This documentary is especially interesting for present purposes, because it contrasts responses to the movie in the modes of what I call Love and Ridicule, and also shows us the different attitudes of the cast and crew towards both types of response.

Troll 2 is in English, even though the director and crew primarily spoke Italian. Indeed, it's reported that no member of the crew was a fluent English speaker except the costume designer. It was filmed in Morgan and Porterville, Utah, with a local cast consisting mostly of nonprofessional actors. The film was written by Fragasso's wife, Rossella Drudi. In *Best Worst Movie*, she explains that she was resentful about many of her friends converting to vegetarianism and wanted to write a vampire movie where vegetarianism replaces vampirism. Thus was born a truly bonkers premise: the town of Nilbog ("Goblin" spelled backwards) is sort of like Salem's Lot, except it's populated by vegetarian goblins instead of vampires. These goblins are given powers by Druid witch Creedence Leonore Gielgud, who draws on the Stonehenge Magic Stone to convert human beings to vegetable matter, which the goblins then consume. As many have noticed, while there are a great many goblins, there aren't actually any trolls in the movie.

The Waits family arranges a home-exchange vacation in Nilbog. Before leaving for the trip, however, young Joshua Waits is visited by the ghost of his grandfather, who warns him that if they eat or drink anything from Nilbog, they will turn into plants and be eaten by goblins. When they arrive at the house, they find a feast waiting for them on the table: ears of corn and crumpets, all smeared with green paste. In a panic to stop his family from eating any of it, Joshua jumps up on the table and pees all over the food. His angry father leads him to his bedroom, and, seeing a series of handwritten signs that had been left to guide them through the house, declares in the movie's most famous line: "Do you see this writing?

Do you know what it means? Hospitality! And you can't piss on hospitality, I won't allow it!"

All hell breaks loose in short order. The abundant goblins in the film wear cheap Halloween masks and burlap sacks as costumes. They feast on fistfuls of slime. The best weapon against the goblin menace turns out to be meat, and, in particular, a double-decker bologna sandwich. It's a veritable orgy of human-plant metamorphoses and green goo. My personal favorite element is the Druid witch Creedence Leonore Gielgud, played by actress and makeup artist Deborah Reed (image 5). She brings a truly inspired level of enthusiasm to the role, cackling and grinning as she delivers lines like: "Now I'm going to welcome our new neighbors. I have just prepared this pudding with wild nettles and a few organic additives to make it delicious and purify the intestines."

Claudio Fragasso did not set out to make a bad film. He began his career making art films and migrated into exploitation movies in a milieu where there was a great deal of overlap between arthouse and grindhouse cinema. For decades,

Image 5: Troll 2 (1990) (Credit: Filmirage)

directors such as Mario Bava and Dario Argento had been making lurid and violent genre movies that nevertheless appealed to the arthouse crowd. Fragasso says in *Best Worst Movie* that, as an Italian, he has a spirit for exaggeration. From his point of view, an over-the-top spectacle like *Troll 2* can at the same time be artistically serious, and with no irony at all he claims: "*Troll 2* is a film that examines many serious and important issues, like eating, living, and dying. It's an important film, which talks about the family, the union of the family, resisting all of those things that want to destroy it and see it dead. People want to eat this family. In Italy, we call this a parable."

Confronted with the reception the movie has received, his reaction is complex. He asserts that some parts of the movie were indeed meant to be funny, but is surprised that audiences laugh at nearly every line. While making the film, the English-speaking cast repeatedly tried to rework the dialogue to better reflect the way Americans actually talk, but Fragasso was insistent that he knows very well how Americans talk and doesn't need any help. As a result of this excess of self-confidence, nearly every bit of dialogue in the movie plays as a joke. Fragasso doesn't mind this. He acknowledges in *Best Worst Movie* that the fans have found qualities that the movie actually has but that he and the film's cast and crew didn't deliberately intend. He says: "This phenomenon helps us to understand that the movie had much more to it than I even knew. More than I knew, more than the writer knew, or the cinematographer or the actors, more than any of us ever knew. Now the movie is saying 'fuck you!' to the critics."

While Fragasso is welcoming of the film's cult of fandom, he bristles at the suggestion that it's a bad movie, let alone the *worst* movie. At the same time, he acknowledges that there is some complexity to the label: "Being considered the worst movie is almost as much of a compliment as being considered the best. It means I've made an impression." The tension in Fragasso's reaction reflects the ambiguity of labeling a movie as "so bad it's good." As I've been arguing, there are at least two very different things this statement can mean. On the one hand, for Bad Movie Lovers, saying that a movie is so bad it's good means that its transgression of received norms is aesthetically appealing. But, on the other hand, for those who approach bad movies in the mode of Ridicule, saying that a movie is so bad it's good means that it's entertaining to make fun of. When Fragasso acknowledges that it's a compliment for the film to be called the worst movie, but then turns around and resists the label, he is reacting to this ambiguity.

The contrast between Love and Ridicule is reflected in the range of attitudes displayed by *Troll 2* fans interviewed in *Best Worst Movie*. One fan muses about what a nice guy *Troll 2* star George Hardy is at conventions: "He's so sincere, he's so genuine. He's exactly why we love *Troll 2*." Hardy is a family dentist with a charming Alabama drawl. He's thrilled when he gets attention from fans. "Honestly, I'm like a cult luminary," he brags to an acquaintance unfamiliar with his acting resume. This dynamic is revealing: there is genuine warmth between many fans of *Troll 2* and the film's cast. These fans aren't interested in mean-spirited jokes at the film's expense; they love it. The same fan who praised Hardy's sincerity later says: "I hope that [Fragasso] understands how wonderful *Troll 2* was, I don't even want to call it a bad film. It's an amazing film." But other fans reveal a less generous attitude. They ask mocking questions such as "what does it feel like to have made the worst film of all time?" While Hardy is jovial enough to play along with questions like this, Fragasso isn't having it: "I think that it's a very good movie. If the others say worst movie, eh, it's their problem, not my problem."

No one could have made a movie as ripe for cult fandom as *Troll 2* by *trying* to make a cult movie. When Rossella Drudi wrote the screenplay, she was really and truly fuming with resentment towards vegetarians. She wasn't trying to be ridiculous, she had the idea of "vegetarians as vampires" and she ran with it. I would recommend watching an interview with her to get a fuller sense of what a character she is. When young Michael reveals that he has armed himself with a double-decker bologna sandwich, Druid witch Creedence Leonore Gielgud exclaims: "Aaahhh! Think about the cholesterol! Think about... THE TOXINS!" It's easy to imagine Drudi grinning with satisfaction as she wrote that line.

But what really puts *Troll 2* over the top is all the glorious acting. The central performances are like lightning in a bottle. The cast aren't making fun of themselves and they aren't making fun of the material. Splattered with green goo, given a script full of gonzo dialogue, and working with a crew that speaks a language they don't understand, they acted their damn hearts outs. Don Packard, a first-time actor who plays the owner of Nilbog's general store (which sells nothing but suspiciously chunky jugs of milk), admits in *Best Worst Movie* that he was stoned during filming and really did not understand what was going on around him. The fear and anxiety his character displays was real. (Side note: around the time he appeared in *Troll 2*, Packard hosted a popular improvised radio show in Salt Lake City under the pseudonym "Golden Delicious." You can still find recordings online.)

The magic of *Troll 2* is its sincerity. It's an earnest collaboration between a director with a spirit for exaggeration, a fiery writer with a bizarre idea, and a cast of eccentric Salt Lake

City locals living out the fantasy of appearing in a feature film. It manifests the absurd conditions of its production and the colorful array of individuals involved, and for this it deserves affection. When confronted with something so immense, I submit that it is small and tawdry to respond with mockery and derision. No joke at the movie's expense could possibly be as funny as the movie itself.

***

Tommy Wiseau's 2003 opus *The Room* is in a league of its own. By all appearances, it is intended as a serious indie melodrama with a tragic conclusion, but it plays as a riotous comedy. From start to finish, it is riven through with utterly ridiculous dialogue, glaring continuity errors, subplots that are introduced but never followed up on, and baffling production design.

While the vast majority of films released in 2003 have faded from memory, *The Room* still sells out midnight showings. Much like *The Rocky Horror Picture Show*, it's inspired a number of audience participation rituals. One prominent set decoration is a picture frame that still holds the stock photo of a spoon that it was sold with. Every time this photo appears onscreen, audience members throw plastic spoons. During a hilariously prolonged shot of a car crossing the Golden Gate Bridge, everyone chants "Go! Go! Go! Go!" When the male characters awkwardly toss a football around (which happens *a lot* in the movie), the audience breaks out the NERF footballs.

It would be hard to imagine how *The Room* got to be the way it is if not for the behind-the-scenes memoir *The Disaster Artist*, co-written by actor Greg Sestero (who plays one of the film's principal characters) and writer Tom Bissell. *The Disaster Artist* was itself adapted into a successful feature film starring James and Dave Franco. I don't care for this film, which feels to me like *The Room* karaoke, but the book is an invaluable supplement. It paints a harrowing portrait of what it was like behind the scenes during the film's calamitous production. While Ed Wood and Claudio Fragasso can readily be seen as endearing, *The Room's* writer, director, and star Tommy Wiseau is a more troubling figure.

Wiseau spent extravagantly on things he didn't need. *The Room* was filmed on 35mm, but he insisted that the crew simultaneously film an HD digital version at great expense, for no reason except to be able to say that it was the first time anyone had done so. He bought rather than rented extremely expensive equipment, apparently in order to shore up the sense that this was a legitimate Hollywood production (ironically, a legitimate Hollywood production would have rented the equipment). He built and rebuilt a set representing a San Francisco rooftop when he actually owned a building in San Francisco with a rooftop that would have been perfect. He had a private bathroom for himself built in the studio, which already had perfectly fine facilities.

But about other things he was infuriatingly cheap. According to Sestero, he refused any suggestion that wasn't his own inspiration. He declined to spend a small pittance to rent a generator, with the result that the crew wasted hours every day coping with power shortages. He did not provide air-conditioning on set, causing one actress to faint and be taken to the hospital. He refused to reimburse a set designer $200 for construction nails, insisting without basis that it was an excessive expense. He paid some crew members well below the going rate, which they accepted on the assumption the film was budget constrained, only to be outraged when they saw the private bathroom and dual-format filming setup.

Wiseau was at once wantonly unprofessional and aggressively intolerant of any behavior he perceived as unprofessional from others. He routinely showed up four hours late and then yelled at anyone he saw taking a break. He made outrageous demands and then berated anyone who questioned them. He made humiliating comments about lead actress Juliette Danielle's body and refused to close the set for marathon filming sessions of *The Room's* ludicrously excessive sex scenes, where she bared her breasts in front of the entire cast and crew while a fully nude Tommy threw rose petals at her and humped her stomach.

In addition to acting in *The Room*, Greg Sestero also has a longstanding friendship (of sorts) with Wiseau and is thus able to offer a litany of details that help illuminate who Tommy is as a person and an artist. He met Tommy in an acting class, where he made a big impression by doing an aggressively over-the-top rendition of Marlon Brando's iconic "Stella!" scene from *A Streetcar Named Desire*. According to Sestero, Tommy cherished nothing more dearly than his far-fetched aspiration to succeed in Hollywood. No one in that acting class could have guessed that he actually had the expansive means and heedless ambition to make it happen, even if his success turned out to be of a very different sort than he hoped for.

By all accounts, Tommy Wiseau is a deeply weird guy. He's suspiciously secretive about his personal history, including his national origin and the source of his wealth. He has long, jet black (dyed) hair and speaks in an unidentifiable accent—vaguely Eastern European but with traces of French. At the time *The Room* was filmed he insisted he was in his 30s, even though he looked closer to 50. He's brazenly arrogant but transparently insecure. He lies incessantly and escalates confrontations unnecessarily. When he goes to a restaurant, he steals other people's reservations and asks to be served a glass of piping hot water immediately, haranguing the wait staff if they treat this as an odd request.

You know how sometimes you meet an exceptionally strange person who wants to tell you all about some grandiose plan they insist they are going to carry out? Perhaps they say they're going to get rich prospecting for gold, or maybe they're carrying around a ragged copy of a screenplay they want to show you: "It's a masterpiece, it will win awards once I find the funding!" *The Room* is what happens when one of these big dreamers is wealthy. The screenplay for *The Room* is the sort of thing that an industry professional would spend at most a few seconds perusing before tossing in the trash can. There is absolutely no way this script gets produced ... unless its author happens to have six million dollars to throw at it, which Tommy, in fact, did.

The combination of Tommy's absolute ineptitude and ample budget is what gives *The Room* its unique qualities. It certainly doesn't look or sound like a six million dollar movie, but amid all of its mistakes and infelicities it has an incongruous polish. Because Tommy could afford to pay real professionals to work on the film, it has a veneer of competence that's hard to reconcile with its fundamental incompetence. This is what puts it in a class of its own: it's too baffling to be a real movie that someone made with serious intentions, but it has some of the trappings of legitimacy.

The Room stars Wiseau as Johnny, a well-off banker who lives with his younger girlfriend, Lisa. Lisa is engaged to marry Johnny, a plan that her mother enthusiastically supports in light of her favorable impression of Johnny's financial standing. But Lisa finds him boring and is attracted to his best friend Mark (played by Sestero). She starts sleeping with Mark, which Johnny eventually discovers. Ultimately, Johnny trashes his bedroom and commits suicide. Surrounding this simple plot arc there is a steady accumulation of outlandish details. The film opens with not one, but *two* production logos, followed by a long stream of credits, including separate credits for each of Wiseau's roles: actor, writer, producer, and director. In the first scene, Johnny walks in the door with a gift for Lisa: a red dress that will figure prominently in the movie. The dialogue is stilted and uncomfortable. One wonders if one is watching an indie drama or a cheap softcore porno. The scene seems to be headed in a steamy direction as Lisa changes into the red dress for Johnny to admire. But then things get *really* uncomfortable when Denny walks in. The character of Denny is one of the oddest elements of the movie. He's supposed to be a teenager who has become a kind of surrogate son to Johnny, but the actor who plays him is in his mid-20s. The audience is given no hint whatsoever at this point about who he is, how he knows Lisa and Johnny, or what he is doing in their house. Lisa and Johnny give him the friendly hint to leave as they head upstairs, implying that they're going to have sex. What happens next is jaw-dropping: Lisa and Johnny get into a pillow fight in their bedroom, and Denny barges in and joins them! Tommy starts tickling him while Lisa hits him with a pillow! This moment is presented as innocent fun, but when they ask him to leave, Denny continues to escalate the creepiness of the situation by explaining: "I just like to watch you guys!" Lisa smiles and laughs and strokes his hair! At this point, the softcore vibe has been disrupted, but when Denny finally does leave, it springs right back as the cheesiest possible slow jam starts playing and the first of the movie's sex scenes commences. It doesn't resemble any actual sex that has ever transpired in all of human history, but there are *a lot* of rose petals involved and we get plenty of looks at Lisa's breasts and Johnny's ashen white ass.

After this auspicious opening, we learn of Lisa's dissatisfaction with Johnny and her attraction to his best friend, Mark. Mark promptly shows up and Lisa sets to work seducing him. As she strokes his hand he inquires: "I mean the candles, the music, the sexy dress, I mean … what's going on here?" The thing is that there are no candles, there's no music, and she's not wearing a dress. But her seduction is nevertheless successful, and the two make love to another cheesy slow jam.

Not long after, Johnny comes home with roses and the bad news that he didn't get an expected promotion, and there's *another* sex scene. But it's not actually a fresh scene, it's a re-edit of the first sex scene, using what appear to be some of the exact same takes. Not long after, another couple, who we have not met yet, show up at Johnny's empty apartment and we get yet *another* sex scene, this time revolving around chocolate and ending in implied fellatio. At this point we are at the 30-minute mark and we are on our fourth sex scene. The sex slows down from here (which is not to say that it stops entirely), but the weirdness continues to escalate. In the middle of an unrelated conversation, Lisa's mother casually tells her that she has breast cancer, a revelation that is never brought up again. In what's unquestionably the best acted scene of the movie, Denny meets a drug dealer named Chris R. on the roof and reveals that he doesn't have the money he owes him. Chris R. pulls out a gun and starts raging: "Where's my fucking money, Denny?!" Lisa, her mom, Mark, and Johnny all burst in and break up the conflict, which feels like it's going to be an important subplot in the movie. It never comes up again.

A full description of *The Room's* bad movie qualifications would require a dedicated book, but suffice to say, they are vast. Pretty much every bit of the movie can play as a joke, even

Johnny's slow-motion suicide, which is immediately preceded by him humping the red dress he gave Lisa at the beginning of the movie. He grunts with each thrust.

How does Wiseau's film fit into the account I've been developing? Part of what's interesting about this case is that unlike *Plan 9 from Outer Space* and *Troll 2*, it's not so clear that the sensibility that *The Room* expresses is worthy of admiration. On one way of looking at it, at least, it's a vanity project by an aggressive, arrogant rich guy who treated his employees abusively. Perhaps mockery is in fact the appropriate response. Doesn't Tommy Wiseau deserve it?

Even if Ridicule is especially justifiable in this case, I still think it's an inferior mode of engagement. My main problem with the practice of ridiculing bad movies for fun is that it's a backhanded way of enforcing restrictive received norms and encouraging to the homogenization of film culture. The behind-the-scenes story of *The Room's* production doesn't change this, although it should have a bearing on our attitude towards Wiseau himself. He should not be unequivocally celebrated as a cult hero the way that some other good-bad auteurs are.

The Room is very much Wiseau's film, but, as *The Disaster Artist* details, it could only be completed because of the titanic efforts of the cast and crew. Experienced script supervisor Sandy Schklair worked tirelessly to give the movie enough continuity to feel like a professional production. The cast and crew suffered through endless shoots and reshoots driven by Wiseau's caprice and incompetence. Throughout the book, Sestero describes the ambivalent attitude that people who worked on the film had towards the prospect of its completion. If it were never completed, they would be spared the embarrassment of being associated with it, but all that labor would be wasted. A lot of talented people worked on the film, paying a huge opportunity cost: they could have been doing something else that might have been more beneficial to their lives and careers. The cult ascendency of *The Room* can be seen as redeeming the hard work and sacrifice that went into the film. The labor of the cast and crew did not go to waste; it resulted in something that makes people happy.

Although Wiseau's treatment of the team that worked on his film is inexcusable, it's not all there is to the man. As Sestero describes him, he's lonely, alienated, and insecure. His arrogant bluster is overcompensation. He wants to be accepted, to have friends, to be a part of the in-crowd, and *The Room* functions as a bizarre form of wish fulfillment. The movie depicts him as being at the center of a social constellation. People show up at his house all the time to toss a football around, see how he's doing, or have sex on his sofa while he's at work. The ending actually does get to a unifying idea for the movie: Johnny was the hub who connected all the other characters. He's easy to take for granted, but without him there is nothing grounding or binding them. When I consider what *The Room* reflects about Tommy's lonely life, I find it doubly sad that he alienated so many of the people who worked on it.

Ultimately, Sestero's primary argument for *The Room* is that it's *sincere*. We can embrace it as such while at the same time denouncing Wiseau's behavior. This is an idea we keep coming back to: one thing the three movies discussed in this chapter have in common is that they are sincere expressions of eccentric artistic sensibilities. At the beginning of the film adaptation of *The Disaster Artist*, there are a few clips of celebrities commenting on *The Room*. The first is from Kristen Bell, who says: "If you were to ask the five best filmmakers in the world right now to make a movie like this, it wouldn't even be in the same universe." You can't fake the level of eccentricity manifested in Wiseau's film. You have to actually *be* that eccentric. There are plenty of good movies out there that were written, directed, and produced by people who know what they are doing. There are too many to watch in a single lifetime. *The Room* is something special and rare: a six million dollar movie by someone who had absolutely no idea what he was doing. He didn't need to *intend* to transgress received norms; he wasn't acquainted with these norms in the first place.

One reason people love the movie is that it creates opportunities for valuable communal experiences ranging from laughs on the sofa with friends to elaborate audience participation rituals. We might worry that such communal practices tend towards mockery of the film. Isn't throwing spoons at the screen inherently a form of Ridicule?

I don't think so. Surely *some* people who go to audience participation screenings of *The Room* are there to make fun of the movie in a mean-spirited way. But this is not essential to the practice, as is plainly obvious when we look at the traditions surrounding the quintessential audience participation movie, *The Rocky Horror Picture Show*. No one goes to see *Rocky Horror* with contempt in their heart; its audience participation rituals are a form of *celebration*. The same is true for *The Room*. Throwing plastic spoons at the screen is a way for audience members to express their shared love for the movie. It's a way for everyone to say to one another: "Seriously, how hilarious is it that they left that spoon picture in the frame and then showed it repeatedly on camera? So hilarious! Let's throw spoons!"

A Beautiful Rainbow of Badness

Three

In the previous chapter, we took a close look at three of the best loved and most iconic good-bad movies. *Plan 9 from Outer Space*, *Troll 2*, and *The Room* are *really* bad. These movies have committed cult followings and well-established reputations. They transgress received norms in such extreme ways that there's absolutely no mistaking them for mainstream consumer products. Embracing them is a way of resisting aesthetic homogeneity and promoting a lively subculture of cult movie fandom. But this subculture risks falling into the grip of an alternative orthodoxy. Film = scholar Daniel Singleton argues that self-styled bad movie fans characteristically insist on *authentic* badness—badness that emerges from a genuine lack of facility with the conventions of mainstream filmmaking.[1] Insistence on this sort of authenticity can be just as stifling as being in the grip of the bland consensus of Rotten Tomatoes critics.

Bad Movie Lovers should steer clear of cool kid countercultural snobbery. In this spirit, we'll turn our attention to a more varied range of titles. Our aim will be to get a broader sense of the types of movie that can be taken as good-bad and the different ways they can be appreciated. It would take more than one book to address the full range of good-bad movies, so I will focus here on some of my personal favorites. Think of it as a bad movie memoir.

DOI: 10.4324/9780367808969-3

First, we'll consider big budget spectacles that were made by experienced professionals and intended as mainstream blockbusters, but that are widely considered to be among the worst movies of all time. Our examples will be *Battlefield Earth* and *Batman & Robin*. I will argue that big, expensive movies of this sort have the potential for a special kind of badness that affords distinctive delights.

Second, we'll take a loving look the apotheosis of 1980s action schlock that was the Cannon Group, as well as the venerable tradition of direct-to-video (DTV) action movies that followed in its wake. In this case, the *genre itself* is transgressive of received mainstream norms. I will argue that this type of action movie has the potential for particular forms of value that depend on the transgressive character of the genre.

***

Sometimes something magical happens when a big budget studio production goes off the rails. Such productions involve vast expense and herculean effort from a massive crew of trained professionals, and so when something does go wrong, the possibility is there for it to go *spectacularly* wrong.

Such was the case for John Travolta's infamous passion project *Battlefield Earth*, based on the first part of the novel with the same title by Church of Scientology founder L. Ron Hubbard. The movie, released in 2000, had a budget of 73 million dollars and was directed by experienced production designer Roger Christian, who won an Academy Award for his work on *Star Wars*. This was not a situation like that in *The Room* or *Plan 9 From Outer Space*, in which the people in charge had no idea what they were doing. This was a legitimate attempt at a box office hit along the lines of such 1990s sci-fi extravaganzas as Roland

Emmerich's *Independence Day*. Indeed, the fact that *Battlefield Earth* is the product of serious efforts by well-funded industry professionals is central to its bad movie appeal: it's pleasantly baffling to consider that they made it this way on purpose. It's no ordinary bad movie: it went on to win not only the Razzie for worst movie of the year, but the special award for the worst drama of the first 25 years of the Golden Raspberry awards.

The first thing that stands out about *Battlefield Earth* is its staggering overuse of Dutch angle shots. A Dutch angle shot is one in which the camera is tilted askew. These shots are typically used to convey a sense of disorientation or psychological disruption. When a character takes hallucinogenic drugs, for instance, the director may use a Dutch angle shot to suggest the disorientation they experience. In *Battlefield Earth*, Roger Christian really and truly goes for it on the Dutch angle shots. They aren't used occasionally for effect, they are the default (image 6). Critic Roger Ebert quipped: "The director, Roger Christian, has learned from better films that directors sometimes tilt their cameras, but he has not learned why."[2]

Battlefield Earth feels strikingly bizarre right out of the gate. The onslaught of Dutch angle shots is so insistent and at the same time so absent of purpose. It's just … a tilted movie. But Christian's inexplicable stylistic choices don't end there. There's also a glaring excess of arty close-ups and gratuitous slow motion shots. It feels as though he's trying to make his directorial voice as ostentatious as possible—he passes up no opportunity for a flourish.

Given that this was a passion project for Travolta, who worked for years to secure funding, one would expect him to give himself a really juicy role to indulge whatever cherished sci-fi fantasies he felt the need to live out. In fact, the role he plays is that of a bumbling, arrogant mid-level

Image 6: Battlefield Earth (2000) (Credit: Franchise Pictures)

bureaucrat seeking professional advancement in the ranks of a species of ten-foot-tall aliens who have colonized Earth for the purpose of resource exploitation. The narrative is a sci-fi adventure story, but the heart of the film is really a satire of bureaucratic incompetence. The self-serving decisions of alien administrators spiral out of control and lead to the destruction of their home planet. As it becomes clearer that this is what the movie is really about, it becomes harder to understand both Travolta's personal zeal for the project and Roger Christian's bombastic stylistic choices. Why are the follies of alien middle management being filmed like a psychedelic fever dream?

Although the movie does get a little exhausting, it is solidly in the realm of good-bad for me. Travolta really leans into his performance, and his over-the-top acting combines with the movie's other excesses to yield something appealingly absurd. In my favorite sequence, Travolta and his associates are trying to gain power over a group of humans, who they refer to as "man-animals" about a thousand times. Their plan is to leave the humans alone and watch them to see which food they seek out first, on this assumption that this will be their favorite food. They plan to then use whatever food this turns out to be as a bargaining chip. But there's no food around! So the man-animals capture and eat a rat. Travolta's character draws a confident conclusion: "We're really going to have leverage over them now! See how much they enjoy rat? How slowly they eat it? Bwa-hahahha!"

Unlike the movies discussed in Chapter 2, *Battlefield Earth* is a well-funded movie made by experienced industry professionals. The lesson we can draw is that bad movie appeal doesn't necessarily depend on authentic incompetence or insufficient means. Here all it really took were some questionable ideas and an excess of enthusiasm. Roger Christian scoffed in the face of restraint and threw in every stylistic exaggeration he could come up with. Travolta approached the role of bumbling alien bureaucrat as if he were playing the marquee villain in a superhero movie. The sublime excess of *Battlefield Earth* couldn't have reached such heights if it were made on the cheap by amateurs. Tens of millions of dollars went into this production, and it shows: it's expensive to be *that* bad. It's important that the ridiculous performance at the center of the film isn't some Joe Schmo, it's John frickin' Travolta, standing ten feet tall, with claws and dreadlocks.

It's no surprise that critics balked. Roger Ebert didn't pull any punches:

> Some movies run off the rails. This one is like the train crash in *The Fugitive*. I watched it in mounting gloom, realizing I was witnessing something historic, a film that for decades to come will be the punch line of jokes about bad movies.[3]

Ebert was right: two decades later, *Battlefield Earth* still gets brought up all the time. But his gloom was misplaced; it's better to be a legendary bad movie than a forgettable good one.

As Claudio Fragasso said in reference to *Troll 2*, when a movie is called *the worst movie of all time*, that means that it made an impression. *Battlefield Earth* has certainly made an impression, and while it may be a bit much for some viewers, it continues to have a place in the bad movie pantheon while so many other titles fade into obscurity.

***

Joel Schumacher's *Batman & Robin* is a different sort of example.[4] Although the film had a strong opening weekend at the box office, its returns rapidly diminished as word of mouth spread and it had a relatively poor domestic showing for a superhero blockbuster. It did even worse with critics and has become a mainstay on lists of the worst movies of all time.

As I write this, Joel Schumacher has recently died and many people (including myself) are revisiting and reconsidering his body of work. He's one of the most prominent openly gay filmmakers in the history of the medium, but he never wanted to draw attention to himself as a trailblazer.[5] Nevertheless, it is clear in retrospect that he was indeed a trailblazer. Throughout his career, beginning at a time when homosexuality was not widely accepted in America, he integrated gay imagery and themes into mainstream film products. This is one of the most interesting dimensions of his work, and a big part of why *Batman & Robin* hit a cultural nerve.

Schumacher took over Warner Brothers' series of Batman films from Tim Burton after the studio decided they wanted to go in a different direction. Burton's films were relatively dark, and some parents complained that they were too violent and sexually suggestive. Warner wanted a family-friendly Batman, with more merchandising opportunities for toys. Schumacher's first installment, *Batman Forever* (which was a commercial success), is certainly less dark and violent than Burton's films, and Jim Carrey's Riddler is a more kid-friendly villain, but Schumacher did *not* tone down the sexuality. Nicole Kidman co-stars as psychologist Dr. Chase Meridian, whose primary traits are intelligence and sexual forwardness. She uses the bat signal to summon Batman to the top of a skyscraper, where she waits for him in high heels and lingerie. She's quite risqué about inviting him for a romantic date: "I'll bring the wine, you bring your scarred psyche."

Batman & Robin picks up where *Batman Forever* left off. In the film's eye-popping opening sequence, Batman (George Clooney) and Robin (Chris O'Donnell) are shown putting on their rubber suits in a rapid series of close-ups. BAM! Batman's ass in tight rubber. BAM! Batman's crotch in a codpiece. BAM! Robin's ass in tight rubber. BAM! Robin's crotch in a codpiece. We are used to seeing female bodies objectified in mainstream films, and we are used to shirtless, hyper-masculine action heroes flaunting their physiques, but this is something different. We don't get a clear look at the face of either hero in Schumacher's opening sequence. What we see are male body parts wrapped in tight rubber, filmed in a blatantly sexual style. This is a glorious example of Schumacher's defiance of the heteronormative expectations that governed blockbuster moviemaking at the time.

Audiences and critics did not approve of the costume work in Schumacher's Batman films. Batman and Robin's suits both have anatomical torsos with six-pack abs and prominent nipples. These bat nipples are usually among the first things mentioned in pans of the film. They became such a persistent subject of disdain that Schumacher came to regret them:

> I just know that I'll always go down over the nipples on Batman … Such a sophisticated world we live in where two pieces of rubber the size of erasers on old pencils, those little nubs, can be an issue. It's going to be on my tombstone, I know it.[6]

Even before he finished making *Batman Forever*, he knew that the costuming decision angered Batman co-creator Bob Kane, and he jokingly told *Premier* magazine: "Bob Kane doesn't understand why Chris O'Donnell [Robin] has an earring and Batman has nipples. I told him 'it's the 90s, Bob! Pumped up!'… I wanted a very sexy, very sensual, very body-hugging suit. It's my Gotham City, and if I want Batman to have nipples, he's going to have nipples!"[7]

Batman & Robin is also disliked for its unrestrained campiness. Camp has its roots in gay subculture and often involves the transgression of dominant gender norms. One of the most famous sequences in the Sternberg/Dietrich films that Sontag cites as paradigms of camp is a big cabaret number in *Blonde Venus*. A performer comes on stage in a full gorilla suit and does a gorilla dance before seductively stripping off her furry mitts to reveal slender, bejeweled hands and then taking off the gorilla mask to reveal … Marlene Dietrich! This is a radical scene in the way it subverts the coding of feminine sex appeal as meek and absent of body hair.

My favorite element of *Batman & Robin* is Uma Thurman's performance as Poison Ivy. She begins the movie as a botanist/nerd in glasses, but is transformed into a sultry supervillain with plant powers after her employer's failed attempt to murder her. Thurman plays Poison Ivy in an Old Hollywood style. She combines Marlene Dietrich's flamboyant hairdos and slinky, languorous way of moving through the world with Mae

West's vampy manner and sassy delivery. In one of my favorite scenes from any superhero movie, Poison Ivy shows up at a black-tie party and does an updated version Dietrich's gorilla suit number from *Blonde Venus*. It's wonderful: Uma Thurman dons a pink, extra fuzzy, poodle-esque gorilla suit and does a sort of sexy gorilla belly dance before stripping off her fuzzy gloves in a shot that recalls Sternberg's original.

Another frequent object of derision in *Batman & Robin* is Arnold Schwarzenegger's campy turn as Mr. Freeze. Schwarzenegger is famous for one-liners such as "I'll be back," and "hasta la vista, baby." *Batman & Robin* blows this shtick up into an entire performance. Not only is pretty much every single thing Arnold says in the movie a one-liner, most of his lines are puns on "cold" or some related word. For example:

> "Allow me to break the ice. My name is Freeze. Learn it well. For it's the chilling sound of your doom."
> "You're not sending me to the cooler!"
> "I'm afraid that my condition has left me cold to your pleas for mercy!"
> "If revenge is a dish best served cold, then put on your Sunday finest. It's time to feast!"

You get the idea. It's very aggressive. Many of these one-liners aren't actually attempts to be funny. They're self-consciously cringey. The joke is cumulative: "How far can we push the corny one-liners past the breaking point?" It's a joke that depends on relating Mr. Freeze to Schwarzenegger's acting career more broadly. It wouldn't make any sense for most actors, but Arnold built his career on his massive physique and dry comic timing. By going way over the top with one-liners, Schumacher inflates the actor's persona to its purest (and therefore campiest) form. This choice is representative of Schumacher's artistic sensibility. Actress Minnie Driver, who appeared in his *The Phantom of the Opera*, reports that on one occasion another actress complained within earshot about how dreadfully over the top she was, and Schumacher glanced up from his newspaper and said in a tone of pity: "Oh, honey, no one ever paid to see under the top."[8] That's exactly the attitude that energizes *Batman & Robin*. It's a mainstream product that's so over the top that it's transgressive. Its transgressive quality directly depends on its status as an attempted blockbuster. It takes a lot of money and the work of a lot of professionals to be as big, loud, and gay as this movie is.

I can't say I'm surprised that most Batman fans reject *Batman & Robin*, as there really isn't very much Batman in the movie and he's not recognizable as the dark, brooding figure that we find in most modern renderings (I mean, it's George Clooney). The storytelling is jumbled and the big set pieces are ridiculously cluttered. *And*, it's over two hours long. Like *Battlefield Earth*, it's a bit exhausting. Despite its mainstream intentions, it's not really a movie for a mass audience. It's a movie for lovers of what Susan Sontag calls "the spirt of extravagance."

In summary, the qualities that Bad Movie Lovers prize are found not just in the works of authentic Hollywood outsiders like those discussed in Chapter 2. Attempted mainstream blockbusters such as *Battlefield Earth* and *Batman & Robin* (and *The Core*, *Catwoman*, *The Island of Dr. Moreau*, its spiritual sequel *Cats*, and countless others) are also capable of transgressing received norms in outrageous ways. It's important for the Bad Movie Lover to avoid the pitfall of countercultural snobbery and disdain for anything too close to the mainstream. Bad Movie Love should be about expanding one's horizons, not narrowing them. We'll take a deeper dive into this issue in

Chapter 4, where we'll consider the way in which Bad Movie Love can break down barriers of elitism and foster mutual appreciation across ordinary cultural divides. But first, we'll consider a category that is very dear to my heart: pulpy action movies.

***

As a child of the 1980s, I grew up on the Cannon Group. I didn't know what that was at the time, but later in life it blew my mind to discover that so many of my childhood favorites were from the same production company. Cannon had been around since the late 1960s as a smaller company that produced exploitation films, but it didn't begin its ascent to legendary status until it was purchased by Israeli cousins Menahem Golan and Yoram Globus in 1979. Golan and Globus had achieved commercial success producing and directing films in Israel, most notably the sex comedy *Lemon Popsicle* and the action drama *Operation Thunderbolt*, starring Klaus Kinski and exploitation queen Sybil Danning. They were lovers of American movies who dreamed of crossing the Atlantic and continuing the success they had achieved in Israel. At the time, the popularity of *Jaws* and *Star Wars* had created a ravenous market for spectacular movies. Golan and Globus bought Cannon and adopted the business model of buying tons and tons of B movie scripts, keeping production costs low, and churning out a glut of big, loud, sleazy pictures in the hope that a few of them turn into hits. They had a spirit of reckless abandon where they would charge forward with basically any idea, no matter how half-baked. This turned out to be unsustainable, but by the time the Cannon Group went under in 1994, they had overseen the release of over

200 films. These movies were all over the map, ranging from Tobe Hooper's comic gorefest *The Texas Chainsaw Massacre 2* to breakdancing musicals *Breakin'* and *Breakin' 2: Electric Boogaloo*, to bawdy skin flicks *Lady Chatterley's Lover* and *Bolero* to attempts to garner highbrow respectability, including Raúl Ruiz's *Treasure Island* and John Cassavetes' masterpiece *Love Streams*.

But make no mistake: the core of Cannon's output was in the action genre. Oh, how I loved their ninja movies as a kid! They inspired me to run around the house with a black t-shirt wrapped around my face like a ninja mask, armed with plastic throwing stars and a plastic katana. *Enter the Ninja*, *Revenge of the Ninja*, *Ninja III: The Domination*, *American Ninja*, *American Ninja 2: The Confrontation*, *American Ninja 3: Blood Hunt*: this stuff is like mother's milk to me. Cannon also produced or distributed a large number of crime, war, and martial arts movies. These include the *Death Wish* sequels, the *Missing in Action Trilogy*, the *Delta Force* series, *Invasion U.S.A.*, *10 to Midnight*, *Cobra*, and three of the films that made Jean-Claude Van Damme a star: *Bloodsport* (i.e., the single most important movie of my childhood), *Cyborg*, and *Kickboxer*.

The Cannon Group has a decidedly mixed reputation. Some of their movies were huge hits, but many others were flops, including some of their most expensive productions (*Over the Top*, *Superman IV: The Quest for Peace*, *Masters of the Universe*). Critics and the media loved to beat up on them and they were widely seen as schlock peddlers. What I want to argue here is that what was good about Cannon and what was seen as bad about Cannon were two sides of the same coin. They embodied the very essence of "so bad it's good."

In the documentary *Electric Boogaloo: The Wild, Untold Story of Cannon Films*, one Golan-Globus associate puts it perfectly: "What they didn't have in taste, they made up for in enthusiasm."

They wanted to make the most over-the-top pictures around, and they had the heedless ambition to pull it off. Their entire approach to making movies was transgressive of received norms. They didn't care about the haters, they were making movies for ordinary folks who wanted to see planes and helicopters blow up and for kids in ninja masks (like me).

Even Cannon's highbrow productions, which are in some cases exceptionally and unequivocally great, owe their special qualities to Golan and Globus' transgressive approach. It can be hard to wrap one's mind around the fact that Cannon is behind both *The Delta Force* and *Love Streams*, but recalling the idea that the good-bad and the avant-garde are both characterized by the transgression of received norms, it begins to make sense. John Frankenheimer, who directed *52 Pick-Up* for Cannon, said that he found it immensely refreshing to work with a producer (Golan) who was himself a director.[9] He and other highly respected directors, such as Franco Zeffirelli, praised Cannon for extending them far more creative freedom than they were used to. Other studios put business first and wanted films free of unnecessary risks, tailored to market trends, and carefully budgeted. Cannon wasn't restrained by this sort of caution. When they did interfere in creative matters, it was typically to ask for more violence and nudity or to promote wild ideas like having Michael "Boogaloo Shrimp" Chambers breakdance on the ceiling in *Breakin' 2* as an homage to Fred Astaire's gravity-defying tap-dance number in *Royal Wedding*. Golan and Globus' willingness to let directors take risks enabled some of the boldest American films of the 1980s.

Cannon's *King Lear*, for instance, is outstandingly abstruse. Its director, none other than Jean-Luc Godard, began his career as one of the core figures of the French New Wave and went on to become one of the most esoteric film artists in the history of the medium. His *Lear* does *not* try to make friends with typical arthouse audiences. Contrary to what these audiences expected and hoped for, it's not really an adaptation of *King Lear* at all, at least not in the usual sense. There are only something like 150 lines of Shakespeare's text spoken in the entire movie. What it's instead about is a post-apocalyptic age brought on by Chernobyl, when all art and culture is dead. One of Shakespeare's descendants seeks to conjure *King Lear* from his ancestral memory and thereby reinvent art. But this is just one thread among many and it's impossible to describe the movie in a way that would convey what it's really like. It begins with a recorded phone call where Menahem Golan berates Godard because he's taking too long making the movie. Godard himself appears as the Professor, wearing a wig made out of RCA cables, microphone cables, phone cords, and other electronic sundries. He talks out of the side of his mouth like Popeye. There's even a fart joke.

Although the film has come to have a favorable reputation with Godard aficionados, it would be a severe understatement to say that it initially baffled audiences. It prompted mass walkouts at early screenings. In a 1994 piece in the *Shakespeare Bulletin* titled "Godard's 'Lear' ... Why Is It So Bad?" David Impastato writes:

> By turns slapstick and funereal, self-mocking and pretentious, Godard's Lear could almost pass for a student movie were it not for some talented presences: Norman Mailer and his daughter Kate, character actor Burgess Meredith, American teen-idol Molly Ringwald, avant-garde opera impresario Peter Sellars, and Woody Allen. The film they populate is so diffuse and unstable that all historical mechanisms of dramatic structure, of tension and release,

> are rendered inoperative. Instead of bursting forth in sudden cataracts or surging in waves, the dramatic energy of Godard's Lear moves across its landscape like a drizzle.[10]

Godard's *King Lear* is a deliberate assault on audience expectations, received norms, and the established institutions of film culture. And how could anyone who had seen Godard's other films from the 1970s and 80s have expected anything else? The deal between Golan and Godard that set the production in motion was inked on a napkin at the 1985 Cannes Film Festival. Can you imagine a deal like this between a major American production company and a director as iconoclastic as Godard in today's movie industry? It's hard to picture anyone but Golan and Globus taking such a risk, and that's what made Cannon special.

Among Cannon's less demanding fare, *Ninja III: The Domination* is a particular favorite of mine. It's the third title in the Ninja Trilogy, which has nothing to unite it except that all three movies involve ninjas and feature Japanese actor Sho Kosugi. By the third movie, Golan wanted to mix things up and asked that a woman be cast as the ninja protagonist. In particular, he wanted Lucinda Dickey (who also starred in Cannon's breakdancing musicals), in spite of the fact that Dickey's background was in dance and *not* martial arts. The team behind *Ninja III* had to figure out some narrative device for explaining how she gets to be a powerful ninja. Their solution is magnificent: she plays a telephone worker and part-time aerobics instructor named Christie Ryder who becomes possessed by the spirit of Black Ninja Hanjuro after she sees him fall in battle while she's out maintaining the phone lines. She takes his supernatural sword home, which later floats and glows neon pink, causing her to go into a trance and carry out ninja assassinations (image 7).

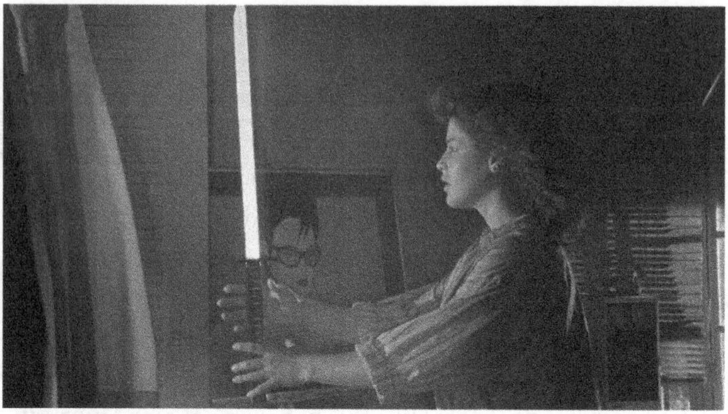

Image 7: Ninja III:The Domination (1984) (Credit:The Cannon Group)

Christie becomes alarmed when she realizes that she's losing large chunks of time to blackouts. She goes to a doctor, who tells her: "There's nothing out of the ordinary, aside from your exceptional extrasensory perception and your preoccupation with Japanese culture. No harm in that!"

Ninja III: The Domination is basically *The Exorcist* meets *Flashdance*, but ninja. The special magic of the movie is that it plays its ludicrous premise straight. It's not making fun of itself. The film's director, Sam Firstenberg, was one of the finest action directors of the 1980s, and his technical work here is impressive by any standard. The film opens with an absolutely astonishing set piece in which the Black Ninja assassinates a scientist who's out playing golf and then undertakes a full-on golf course massacre, killing everyone in sight and then too many responding police officers to count. Firstenberg directs the entire movie with skill and panache, never treating it like the silly trifle it might have been. *Ninja III* embodies what's great about Cannon: they took an absurd idea that no business-minded studio executive would have given a moment of serious consideration and carried it out with unflinching gusto.

***

Cannon is irreplaceable. No other production company could give us both Godard's *King Lear* and *Ninja III: The Domination*. But the spirit of Cannon lives on in the grand tradition of direct-to-video (DTV) genre cinema. Production companies such as PM Entertainment and Action International Pictures sprang up in the late 1980s and flooded the VHS rental market with low-budget genre movies. In 1992, Cannon associates Avi Lerner and Boaz Davidson founded Nu Image, a company that produced huge numbers of low-budget action movies for DTV release. These movies were often filmed in Bulgaria or South Africa and starred B movie stalwarts like former World Light-heavyweight Kickboxing Champion Gary Daniels or 1980s action stars such as Dolph Lundgren. Nu Image was successful during the 1990s, but today the studio is best known for its subsidiary labels, Millennium Films and Millennium Entertainment, which produced mid-budget projects intended for theatrical release beginning in the mid-2000s, including the *Expendables* and *Has Fallen* series, a number of Jason Statham and Nicolas Cage vehicles, and a grab bag of eccentric projects including Lee Daniels' sleazy Florida noir *The Paperboy* (a personal favorite). Millennium Films has been sold and renamed as Millennium Media, but it's still in business.

There is an enduring appetite for this style of movie. One might find that fact a little curious, given that DTV action movies have a terrible reputation with critics and the general public. Although there are exceptions, you'll be hard pressed to find many DTV action titles with favorable Rotten Tomatoes or IMDB scores. Given that there are more critical and popular hits out there than most people have time to watch, who is spending precious hours watching reams and reams of low-budget action movies?

Me, for one. As an avid lover of the action genre, I actively prefer DTV to most of what gets released in theaters nowadays. Film critic Ignatiy Vishnevetsky makes an insightful case for this stance in his piece, "Today's best action directors aren't working in Hollywood, but in direct-to-video"[11] He writes:

> At their core, action movies are about bodies—bulging veins, swelling muscles, chests and foreheads drenched with sweat—and what those bodies are capable of. When there's a sense of unity between what the body is doing and what the camera is doing, the result can be sublime. A body framed a certain way becomes figurative art and takes on a meaning that goes beyond the context of narrative or character. Space becomes sculptural, and movement becomes musical. That's the essence of what made action movies a vital, exciting genre to begin with. Hollywood seems to have lost that sensibility, but in the direct-to-video world, it remains as striking as ever.

There are certain qualities that mainstream critics and audiences have come to expect and demand from action movies that are not essential to the genre, including prolonged character development, dramatic weight, extensive world-building, plot rationality, grandiose effects, elaborately detailed production design, and (often) a link to a preexisting franchise. There's nothing wrong with these features in themselves and there is certainly a place for them, but it is detrimental to the action genre to treat them as requirements, because they are sometimes incompatible with other desirable qualities that are distinctive of the genre. As Vishnevetsky vividly conveys, action is capable of a special sort of beauty that depends on *minimalism*. Some of the very best action sequences in all of cinema consist in nothing more than a creatively framed and fluidly edited clash between fighters. As classic martial arts films such as *Golden Swallow* and *The Eight Diagram Pole Fighter* illustrate, the best action choreography is capable of the same sort of musical rhythms and graceful elegance that we prize in dance choreography. When action movies are too laden with narrative and character or cluttered with effects, the virtues of minimalism are lost.

Minimalist action movies can feel cheap and shoddy in contrast to Hollywood productions, but this is part of their appeal. Critic Pauline Kael writes: "[A]udiences who have been forced to wade through the thick middle-class padding of more expensively made movies to get to the action enjoy the nose-thumbing at 'good taste' of cheap movies that stick to the raw materials. At some basic level they like the pictures to be cheaply done, they enjoy the crudeness; it's a breather, a vacation from proper behavior and good taste and required responses."[12] This is not to say that *every* action movie should be minimalistic; there's also a place for the union of grandiose spectacle and emotional drama. The issue is that the lack of middle-class padding is seen as an inherent flaw, which relegates minimalistic action movies to a disreputable niche. But the beauty of disreputable niches is that with low stakes comes great freedom. Because they are produced so cheaply, DTV action movies don't have to appeal to a broad audience in order to be profitable. Fans of MMA and professional wrestling, 1980s nostalgists, action fiends, and open-minded cinephiles such as Vishnevetsky together constitute a large enough group to sustain the DTV market. Directors are free to abandon concern for received mainstream norms and cater to this niche audience. It is therefore entirely predictable that the movies that DTV fans most highly prize will tend to have poor Rotten Tomatoes and IMDB scores. These movies are transgressive in their very conception: they aren't trying to satisfy received norms, win awards, please critics, or score big at the box office. They are trying to appeal to a small but devoted audience by fitting into the tradition of genre cinema that is directly descended from the Cannon Group. The best contemporary DTV action directors—a list that includes Isaac Florentine, Jesse V. Johnson, Roel Reiné, and John Hyams—have produced a large and varied body of work that successfully exploits the freedom afforded by the format. Highlights include fighting movies such as the *Undisputed* sequels, Cannon-esque oddities such as *U.S. Seals II: The Ultimate Force* and *Bridge of Dragons*, and sleazy exploitation movies such as *Death Race 2*.

I'm fond of DTV action movies in part because of the way they tend to shed the clutter of character and narrative. It's ingrained in mainstream critical taste that for a story to be engaging, the narrative must not follow a standard formula too closely, and we must become interested in the characters and what happens to them. But why does *every* movie have to be this way? Formulaic narratives and superficial characterizations may not be conducive to engaging stories but *there are other ways in which a movie can be distinct and interesting*. I've already mentioned the beauty of minimalist action, but the DTV action genre has many other special qualities. These movies often substitute *persona* for character. We don't need to spend a lot of time getting to know a character if that character is played by Jason Statham. Statham comes with a built-in persona. This feature of DTV action provides an opportunity for connoisseurship:

by watching lots and lots of Statham movies one can gain a very fine-grained appreciation of the subtle shades of Statham.

I think of formulaic narratives in much the same way as classical subject matter for paintings. There are a whole lot of paintings of the Virgin Mary and the baby Jesus. Art historians don't disparage these works because of their repetitive subject matter. Paintings that are very similar in composition can still differ greatly with respect to style and emotional resonance. The same is true of formulaic action movies. Two movies about a team of mercenaries rescuing a diplomat from an international terrorist might follow nearly the same narrative path but be entirely different with respect to action choreography and cinematic style. The formulaic nature of low-budget action cinema is a feature, not a bug.

Literary scholar Thomas J. Roberts has developed a theory of the appeal of junk fiction that is helpful. He writes:

> In reading any single story, then, we are reading the system that lies behind it, that realizes itself through the mind of that story's writer. And here lies the fundamental distinction between reading one book after another and reading in a genre, between reading with that story focus and reading with the genre focus. Genre reading is system reading. That is, as we are reading the stories, we are exploring the system that created them.[13]

Different people look for different things in genre cinema, but certainly a big part of the appeal for me and many others is the opportunity genre movies afford for the sort of systematic engagement that Roberts describes. For the most part, I'm not watching DTV action movies for their stories. There are plenty of movies with good stories. I started getting interested in the genre because I enjoy the sort of minimalist aesthetic discussed above and because I like the laconic wit of action movie dialogue and the charisma of performers such as Scott Adkins and Jean-Claude Van Damme. As I dug deeper, I became interested in *the genre itself*. That is, I became interested in the system of character archetypes, plot formulae, etc. that lies behind any given movie in the genre.

Today, when I watch something like Charles Band's delightful 1991 sci-fi action flick *Trancers II: The Return of Jack Deth*, I engage with it in part by relating it to the system that lies behind it. There's a whole *Trancers* extended universe—actually, it's a multiverse—that we explore across six feature films and one short, and this multiverse is connected with other fictional worlds under the broader umbrella of Full Moon Features (the B movie production company behind the series). *Trancers* is about Jack Deth, a timecop, traveling back to the 1980s to prevent telepathically possessed trancers from assassinating the ancestors of the governing council of the 23rd century. There's an elaborate mythology that adds flesh to the fictional world, and this mythology gets increasingly arcane as the series progresses. In *Trancers* 6, Jack Deth (now inhabiting the body of a young woman) summarizes the state of affairs: "These time travel paradoxes have finally gone from the ridiculous to the sublime."

When I watch *Trancers II*, I don't just engage with it directly, I also view it in connection with the broader categories that it belongs to, including the subgenre of movies about timecops and the filmography of Full Moon Features. I focus on similarities and differences between the particular movie I'm engaging with and other entries in these categories. The protagonist of the *Trancers* series, Jack Deth, combines elements of Philip Marlowe, Dirty Harry Callahan, and Rick Deckard (from *Blade Runner*), which invites the viewer to think about Tim Thomerson's performance in connection these iconic characters and their various iterations. The villain of *Trancers II* is a time-travelling telepathic terrorist posing as an environmental activist, played by the great Richard Lynch. When I see him in this sort of role, I don't view his performance in isolation; I view it against the pantheon of great Richard Lynch villains, which include his unforgettable role in Larry Cohen's *God Told Me To* and his turns in Cannon Group films such as *The Sword and the Sorcerer*, *Invasion USA*, and *The Barbarians*. What's interesting about any given Richard Lynch villain is bound up with that character's relation to Lynch's persona and his larger body of work. It's thrilling to me, for example, to consider the similarity between the way he plays evil usurper Titus Cromwell in *The Sword and the Sorcerer* and the way he satirizes cultish activist leaders in *Trancers II*. There's a particular Richard Lynch brand of evil, and it's fascinating to see it deployed in such a diverse range of contexts.

Perhaps the most expansive opportunity in American action cinema for systematic engagement is the "*Die Hard* scenario" subgenre. The success of *Die Hard* has inspired many, *many* copycats. It is the Madonna and Child of the action genre. The two most iconic examples are *Under Siege*, which is "*Die Hard* on a boat" with Steven Seagal in the Bruce Willis role and Tommy Lee Jones in the Alan Rickman role, and *Sudden Death*, which is "*Die Hard* at a hockey game" with Jean-Claude Van Damme as Willis and Powers Boothe as Rickman. But there are so many more! There's a website called "The *Die Hard* scenario Wiki" that describes itself as "a collaborative website dedicated to sharing information about the films related to the concept of *Die Hard*, which revolutionized the action genre and led to the creation of movies that have the scenario of *Die Hard*."[14] There are *hundreds* of movies on the site, and browsing through the list and contemplating why someone decided to add a given title raises interesting questions about what it is to be a *Die Hard* scenario movie. *Under Siege* and *Sudden Death* are obvious, but how far does the category go? There's a page on the wiki that lists science fiction examples. I am very impressed by whoever figured out that *Skyline* is a *Die Hard* scenario movie, and also quite intrigued by the suggestion that *Star Trek: First Contact* should count. That makes me want to see it again. The point, at any rate, is that I don't just engage with particular *Die Hard* scenario movies; I engage with the larger system. This form of engagement is interesting in much the same way that other types of systematic aesthetic engagement are interesting.

Food is a great example.[15] On my last trip to NYC, I had slices at eight different pizzerias. I didn't simply attend to the intrinsic qualities of each slice; I also compared them to one another and related them to my idea of what the relevant style of pizza should be like. I found it interesting to think about how to rank the slices from best to worst, and what criteria I should use. This led me to further clarity about my own preferences: I like crust that's crispy on the bottom and quite thin, but not so thin that it lacks a nice, toothsome chew. I don't like sugar in pizza sauce, but one of the most prominent styles of NYC pizza standardly contains sugar. Should I factor my preference into my evaluations or should I take sweet sauce as essential to the category and try to bracket it? Attending to this sort of question adds a systematic dimension to my engagement with a particular slice. Writer Colin Atrophy Hagendorf took this form of engagement to its furthest extreme when she tried slices from *every single pizzeria on the island of Manhattan*, reviewed them all, selected her favorites, and then wrote a book about it called *Slice Harvester: A Memoir in Pizza*. This is, so to speak, *eating in a system*, and it has the same basic structure as engaging with umpteen *Die Hard* scenario movies in a systematic manner. I suggested in Chapter 1 that the ultimate value of artworks consists in their capacity to sustain valuable activities of engagement. I propose that genres and subgenres can have such a capacity in their own right. *Die Hard* scenario movies are a dime a dozen, and any given example of the subgenre doesn't necessarily hold much interest on its own, but the subgenre itself is fascinating, and each title becomes more interesting when viewed in the context of the larger system.

Up to this point in the book, most of the examples of good-bad movies we have discussed are good-bad in virtue of being *outrageous*, *absurd*, *over the top*, and so on. While this is true of many DTV action movies as well, the qualities that are most distinctive of the genre are that it's *cheap*, *disposable*, *shoddy*, *formulaic*, *derivative*, *lacking in three-dimensional characters*, and so on. These qualities are conventionally negative, but, in this context, they have the potential to be appealing. The formulaic nature of action narratives keeps the middle-class padding to a minimum and affords the opportunity for systematic engagement. Cheapness comes in many shades, and some of them are delightful.

***

Most DTV titles have at most a small handful of reviews on Rotten Tomatoes, but it is very telling to peruse the larger set of reviews that bona fide DTV hits sometimes garner. One of the most revered DTV titles is John Hyams' *Universal Soldier: Day of Reckoning*. Critic R. Emmet Sweeney, writing for highbrow cinephile magazine *Film Comment*, recognizes that it is a special film:

> For the sixth entry in a formerly moribund direct-to-video cyborg franchise, *Universal Soldier: Day of Reckoning* is

> a remarkably ambitious movie. Wrestling with the malleable nature of identity in between ingeniously choreographed brawls, it's both a head trip and an adrenaline rush ... Hyams has created a truly unique object, a horror-action-flicker film about uniquely expressive bodies haunted by the minds and memories they are forced to house.[16]

The original 1992 *Universal Soldier* is a schlocky sci-fi actioner/fish-out-of-water comedy about a military cyborg trying to fit in among humans. *Day of Reckoning* is really nothing like it; it's a hallucinatory bloodbath with complex themes of memory and personal identity. Many commentators consider it an exceptional artistic achievement. Nevertheless, the film is certified rotten on the Tomatometer and many of its negative reviews dismiss it out of hand on account of its pedigree. For example, Scott Bowles, writing for *USA Today*, pans the film as though it were obviously bad simply in virtue of being a *Universal Soldier* sequel:

> Universal soldiers, it seems, never die, even if they deserve a slow and deliberate farewell. Witness *Universal Soldier: Day of Reckoning* ... the latest incarnation of a low-budget franchise that has been churning out stinkers for 20 years. Despite treating its women as props, blood as canvas and Jean-Claude Van Damme and Dolph Lundgren as actors, this never-ending story of dead Vietnam war soldiers reincarnated to become turbo-killers has expelled mindless installments to theaters and video shelves since 1992. Reckoning would be a fitting epitaph to the franchise, as it embraces all of the anger and head-turning violence of the series. But this movie suggests no visible end for our

> heroes Luc Deveraux (Van Damme) and Andrew Scott (Lundgren), whose biceps remain more expressive than their faces.[17]

Needless to say, I am unimpressed by this take. The film successfully combines the visceral satisfactions of the action genre with bracing formal experimentation and heady arthouse themes. It achieves an extraordinary level of immersive, nightmarish atmosphere, especially relative to its budget. It would be one thing to put together a thoughtful negative critique of the film, but Bowles' review is lazy. "Of course it's bad; it's a *Universal Soldier* sequel." This isn't film criticism so much as the smug expression of a desiccated imagination, devoid of insight or vision.

From the point of view of a lover of the action genre or a sympathetic cinephile, *Universal Soldier: Day of Reckoning* is plainly great. But there is a wide chasm between such fans and most critics who work for major publications like *USA Today*. The films that ardent genre fans most intensely admire are more often than not met with dismissive mockery by mainstream critics. In this way, DTV action is a *good-bad genre*: it is prized by its fans in virtue of the ways it transgresses received norms. The elements of DTV action films that fans value are often the very same elements that mainstream critics and audiences haughtily mock. What a critic like Bowles sees as mindless violence, a fan might see as graceful brutality unencumbered by sentimentality and unnecessary dramatic baggage. What Bowles sees as wooden acting, a fan might see as a stoical invocation of the actor's persona. DTV action is a good-bad genre because its intended audience is a niche of viewers with taste that is in conflict with received norms. As Kael puts it: "The lowest action trash is preferable to wholesome family entertainment.

When you clean them up, when you make movies respectable, you kill them. The wellspring of their art, their greatness, is in not being respectable."[18] The qualities that give cheap action movies a bad reputation are often exactly what people like Kael and myself love about them.

There are plenty of other good-bad genres: nunsploitation, sex comedy, cannibal horror, peplum ... the list goes on. These categories are not for everyone, but they do offer special and distinctive qualities. The key to engaging with good-bad genres is to meet them on their own terms. Exploitation movies in general trade in various forms of transgressive spectacle and are unconcerned with niceties of plot and character. I greatly enjoyed the recent road rage exploitation movie *Unhinged*, in which Russell Crowe plays an aggrieved asshole on a murderous rampage. The pleasure this movie offers is very specific: you know Russell Crowe, you associate him with a certain type of respectable performance where he plays an authority figure or romantic hero (or occasionally a math genius or Noah from the Old Testament). But now here he is, giving one of the most transgressive performances of his career. The gleeful shock of seeing him in such a beastly role is all I need from this movie. A friend watched it on my recommendation and complained afterwards that the plotting didn't make any sense. Why does it take so long for the cops to come? Why do they keep sending only one cop? Why doesn't the main character do the most prudent thing at every juncture?

Hitchcock had a name for viewers who approach films this way: the Plausibles. To these viewers, every motivation and plot development must be explained in a way that's consistent and transparent to the audience. If a movie fails at plausibility, it fails in total. I've always had trouble imagining why anyone would look at movies this way, but, alas, they do. The account of good-bad genres that I've suggested explains what they are doing wrong: they are importing norms from the mainstream into genres that play by different rules. *Unhinged* doesn't give a damn about getting the procedures of the LAPD right or presenting every character as doing the most rational thing at every juncture. It's about Russell Crowe crashing cars and smashing faces. If you're not into that, that's fine, there are plenty of movies that spend half their running time explaining the rules and confirming that everything in the plot checks out. But please don't insist that every movie has to be this way. It would be an awful shame if every movie were bogged down by the logistics of plausibility and there were no space for recklessly trashy spectacles like *Unhinged*.

***

Returning to *Universal Soldier: Day of Reckoning*, the contempt that Scott Bowles and other critics show for Jean-Claude Van Damme and Dolph Lundgren as actors is especially revealing. Received norms concerning what counts as good acting are among the most stifling and pernicious of all. Mainstream critics and gatekeeper institutions such as the Academy Awards are in the grips of an impoverished idea of what good acting looks like. Method acting, naturalism, and convincing transformations are excessively prized while more mannered or minimalistic acting styles are underappreciated. Deriding Lundgren and Van Damme for a lack of facial expressiveness reflects an unduly narrow outlook. Consider Clint Eastwood's iconic performances as the Man with No Name in Sergio Leone's Dollars Trilogy. His laconic acting is a big part of what makes those movies so great. Would his performances have been improved by more dynamic facial expressions? No!

Van Damme and Lundgren are both fascinating people. Van Damme's biography is well known: he began his career in Belgium as a body builder with a background in martial arts and ballet and eventually became a huge international star thanks to his jaw-dropping splits, graceful 360 crescent kicks, boyish good looks, and charming accent. He was like the Fred Astaire of 1980s action. Fewer people know Dolph Lundgren's incredible life story. After growing up in Sweden, he became a successful chemical engineering student. While studying for his master's degree at the University of Sydney in Australia he did some competitive fighting and worked as a bouncer and bodyguard for performers at a popular venue. On one occasion, he protected none other than Grace Jones, with whom he then became romantically involved. He won a prestigious Fulbright scholarship to attend MIT, but after only a few weeks he dropped out to live with Jones in NYC. He became part of the hip 1980s NYC art scene and hung out at Andy Warhol's factory. He and Jones were the subject of a number of photographs by Warhol himself. His acting career began when he appeared along with Jones in *A View to a Kill*. He had his breakthrough when he was cast as Ivan Drago in *Rocky IV* not long after.

Both Lundgren and Van Damme saw the peak of their popularity in the 1980s and 90s before going on to have long, prolific careers in low-budget action movies. While their later films are uneven in quality, the high points are very high. Both actors have unique and striking faces, and their distinctive features have only gotten more pronounced as they've aged. Both also still have stunning physiques, with chiseled musculature showing through weathered skin. Critic Stephen Holden once aptly describe Lundgren as a "massive kinetic sculpture."[19] He and Van Damme continue to this very day to use their physical attributes to great effect, often playing grizzled, aging tough guys beset with melancholy.

In the 2018 film, *The Bouncer*, for instance, Van Damme plays a widower who has gone into hiding in Belgium with his young daughter after dark and mysterious events forced him to flee South Africa. He gets entangled with organized crime after taking a job as a bouncer at a strip club. When his daughter is threatened, he must once again turn to violence. Van Damme's exceptional performance carries the film. Tracking shots set to a throbbing, bass-heavy score follow him through seedy nocturnal spaces. His body language suggests that he's carrying the weight of a lifetime of loss and regret as he trudges forward to do the next brutal, necessary thing (image 8).

Much of Lundgren's DTV work is similarly compelling, although he tends towards lighter fare than Van Damme does. Some people, including me, will watch *any* movie with Dolph Lundgren in it. I watched *Kindergarten Cop* 2. Sometimes this doesn't work out very well. Lundgren has undoubtedly appeared in some stinkers, like the low-budget *Die Hard* scenario movie

Image 8: The Bouncer (2018) (Credit: Blue Fox Entertainment)

Hard Night Falling, which doesn't have very much going for it on even the most generous estimation. Even when viewed in connection with the larger system, it's only interesting as an example of a particularly uninspired *Die Hard* scenario movie. The vast majority of the time, however, when Dolph is on the screen, he dishes up something worthwhile (I actually sort of like *Kindergarten Cop 2*). Anyone who has only seen his most famous performances would be surprised both by his range and his quirky eccentricity. In the 2015 WWII movie *War Pigs*, for example, he plays a French legionnaire named Captain Hans Picault, who is tasked with training a group of defiant American soldiers how to fight behind enemy lines. He leans into his hammy French accent as he delivers some delectable dialogue:

> "Zee art of the knife. It's a deadly art."
> "There is more to knife fighting than fighting with knives."

His filmography really is a treasure trove. In the 2009 thriller *Command Performance*—which he co-wrote and directed—he plays a jaded, shirtless, stoner drummer with spiked blonde hair who lives in Moscow and plays in a Russian rock band while hiding a dark and violent past. When the Russian premier is taken hostage at a concert Lundgren has just performed at, he has to return to his violent ways and save the day. It's another *Die Hard* scenario movie, but this time it's a great one. He wrote some choice dialogue for himself: "Dying's easy; rock and roll is hard." Or, in the 2016 DTV horror movie *Don't Kill It*, he plays Jebediah Huntley, a demon hunter with a twangy southern accent who wears a duster and VAPES. I would eagerly watch five sequels featuring this character.

When DTV action fans who are familiar with the latter-day work of Lundgren and Van Damme watch *Universal Soldier: Day of Reckoning*, we don't see two over-the-hill actors carrying on with some worthless 1990s franchise. Rather, we see two legends reprising iconic roles in a movie that embraces the larger system it emerges from while at the same time demonstrating bold artistry. It's a direct-to-video masterpiece, and it enables especially valuable activities of engagement for viewers who are able to situate it in its proper context.

We'll return to the topic of acting in Chapter 5, where we'll take a close look at the career of Nicolas Cage. First, however, you're going to have to hear all about my personal journey with *Twilight*.

Taste and *Twilight*

Four

I love the *Twilight* movies. Full stop.

It took me a while to get there. I've always loved vampires, but *Twilight* initially repelled me. I resented the way that Stephanie Meyer cashed in on the dark appeal of the undead by stripping away anything too threatening or unsettling and doubling down on wish fulfillment. I thought of it as defanged vampire fare for starry-eyed YA readers susceptible to the chaste tantalization of Meyer's heavy-handed abstinence parable.

I felt territorial about vampire lore:

> "Hey, kids, when vampires go in the sunlight they don't sparkle like diamonds, they are incinerated in a fiery blaze."
> "Vampires don't play baseball."
> "Why are the Cullens so hung up on meek human morality? Feast upon this mortal!"

I was content to disdain *Twilight* and leave it at that. My change of heart was set in motion a decade ago, when my brother called me and breathlessly reported: "Dude, I just watched *Twilight: New Moon* and it is WILD. There is so much bad wolf CGI. You've gotta see how bad these wolves look. The dialogue is so great. Just see it, I know you didn't like the first one, but this actually makes me like it more in retrospect."

DOI: 10.4324/9780367808969-4

I took his recommendation, and I was not disappointed. *New Moon* is indeed amazing. Incel werewolf Jacob Black tries to win Bella's love by never wearing a shirt and adopting an entitled posture while she pines for a vampire who's obsessed with sexual purity. Meanwhile, her vampire beau Edward decides that the best way to protect her from another vampire's blood vendetta is to travel far enough away that he wouldn't be able to get back in time to save her from an attack.

It contains lines like:

> "If this is about my soul, take it! I don't want it without you."
>
> "Victoria won't be happy about me killing you. But I can't help myself. You're so mouth-watering."
>
> "Alice, is it possible that *everything* is true?"

Drawn in by all this silliness, I rewatched the first movie and found that it has similar bad movie charms. But with my newly sympathetic gaze, I also found that it has a lot of conventionally admirable qualities that I missed the first time around. It's directed by Catherine Hardwicke, who previously demonstrated her sensitive attunement to teenage emotional life in her films *Thirteen* and *Lords of Dogtown*. Most of the movie is ludicrous (in a way I now appreciate), but it also has a sprinkling of well-realized quieter moments. In particular, Hardwicke has a deft touch with the interplay between fear and lust. Edward and Bella desire one another intensely, but Edward is afraid that if he lets himself get carried away by his attraction he will lose control and drain her blood. Bella finds this danger arousing. Hardwicke's framing in these scenes is dreamy and graceful. Indeed, these scenes could fit into a highbrow art film, but that can be hard to recognize when the next scene is vampire baseball (image 9).

Image 9: *Twilight* (2008) (Credit: Summit Entertainment)

I like all of the *Twilight* films, but my favorite is easily *Breaking Dawn – Part 1*, which begins with Bella and Edward's picture-perfect wedding and ends with a harrowing vampire pregnancy bloodbath. It's a very worthy entry in the venerable pregnancy horror subgenre, which includes classics such as *Rosemary's Baby* and *Alien* as well as newer titles like the 2007 French horror movie *À l'intérieur*. I'm not impressed by the majority of critical takes on *Breaking Dawn – Part 1*. Even reviews that praise the horror finale—which really is excellent by any standard—tend to reject the earlier part of the film. James Berardinelli, for instance, writes: "Here's hoping *Breaking Dawn – Part Two* gives us more of what *Part One* provided in the final 30 minutes than what it forced viewers to endure to get there." I think this is a mistake. The power of the finale depends on the progression of the film as a whole. *Breaking Dawn – Part 1* has a tighter focus than the other entries in the series, which jump around between multiple subplots. This time, we focus on a linear series of events: Bella and Edward get married; they go on their honeymoon; they have sex for the first time; Bella becomes pregnant; she gives birth. The simplicity of the narrative is important; the movie is about the jarring way that fantasy can give way to reality. The wedding sequence and the first part of the honeymoon enact the fantasy of marrying a dangerous but nonthreatening immortal vampire with an unbeating heart full of infinite devotion. What I find especially compelling about the film is the way the nightmarish ending relates to the dreamy wish fulfillment that precedes it. Bella has been trying to get into Edward's pants since the first movie, and when she finally attains the forbidden fruit of vampire sex, she *immediately* finds herself with a supernaturally rapid pregnancy. The entire gestation takes two weeks, during which the human-vampire hybrid she carries saps her life energy and renders her frightfully emaciated. Meanwhile, Edward is at a loss. He gets on the internet and googles something to the effect of "vampire baby." We then see a montage of gruesome search results, including a few of Francisco Goya's Black Paintings (!). As Bella's condition worsens, her caretakers suggest that she try drinking some blood, which does indeed help. The image of Kristen Stewart drinking blood through a straw is memorable, but not as memorable as what follows: Edward giving her a Caesarian section *with his fangs*. The horror of the film is effective because we move so briskly from "ooh this is the perfect honeymoon" to Edward ripping his unholy spawn from Bella's womb with his teeth. *Breaking Dawn – Part 1* makes vivid the way our most cherished fantasies can be laced with abject terror at the prospect of their fulfillment. It is surprising and potent because it takes such a sharp turn from the lightness of the earlier movies. It fulfills the sense of longing that pervaded those movies, but it doesn't let the gratification of this fulfillment linger even for a single day of Bella's life.

One might object that I've just described a sexist parable where a woman is punished for having sexual desires. I strongly disagree. It's a horror movie, and a horror movie can reflect a prominent fear without endorsing the cultural context that grounds it. It goes without saying that fears about pregnancy are prominent among young women. In any case, *Twilight* doesn't ultimately punish Bella for her desires—she gets an eternity of hot vampire sex. But it saves this happy ending for *Breaking Dawn – Part 2*, and the split benefits *Part 1* by letting it function as a self-contained horror movie that centers a prominent fear of its intended audience.

***

At least in my circles, it's cool to like *The Room* and it's cool to like *Troll 2*, but it's decidedly uncool to like *Twilight*. I can't just casually let slip that I'm a *Twilight* fan. People invariably ask: "You mean you like making fun of it, right?"

But the thing is that I would never make fun of it. I adore *Twilight*. Do I think it's bad? Yes, by conventional standards, most of it is bad. But it's bad in a good way—a way that I sincerely cherish. And I think some parts of it are conventionally good.

Sometimes, I explain all this. But most of the time I just nod: "Yes, I like making fun of it." It's a lie that I tell to avoid having to litigate my actual stance, which is that *Twilight* is awesome. I don't enjoy litigating this stance because most of my interlocutors don't take it seriously. They assume that I'm just taking the joke a level further by pretending to like *Twilight* sincerely.

This dynamic reveals something deep about the nature of taste and the way it functions in the aesthetic and social dimensions of our lives. In what remains of this chapter, I'll use the case of *Twilight* to examine two connected issues. The first is the way that taste functions as a form of self-expression, and, in particular, as a way to affiliate ourselves with some groups of people while distancing ourselves from others. The second is whether it's really possible to like a movie because it's bad without engaging in what I've been calling Ridicule.

The reason widespread disdain for *Twilight* is so presumptive and harsh, I suggest, is that the franchise is seen as being for people with naïve, undeveloped taste—in particular, adolescent girls. There's no doubt a lot of misogyny wrapped up in this disdain, and it's focused on the particular sense that adolescent girls have bad taste and that works of art made with the narrow aim of appealing to them shouldn't appeal to other groups of people who don't have the excuse of being adolescent girls.

Scholar Jacqueline M. Pinkowitz has published an article in which she examines the internet activities of the Anti-Twilight Movement.[1] The Anti-Twilight Movement is a loosely organized collective with a website full of gendered indictments of *Twilight* fans: they're hysterical, hyperemotional, and prone to shrieking fits. These anti-fans go to great lengths to build a case against *Twilight*. According to Pinkowitz, they feign concern about the dangers of *Twilight*'s positive depiction of male possessiveness and abusive relationship dynamics, as though it can be taken for granted that young female fans are unreflective about these elements of the fiction and prone to passively absorb and emulate them.

Although the Anti-Twilight Movement is an extremist faction, their platform is on a continuum with more typical disdain for the series. One reason that it's easy for my peers to accept that I like *Troll 2*, but hard for them to accept that I sincerely love *Twilight*, is that *Twilight* is seen as being *for girls*, and I'm a 40-year-old straight guy with a beard and tattoos. My fondness for *Twilight* doesn't fit with the way the franchise is coded in our culture. It has significant fandom among gay men and gender nonconforming people, but it's just not something that a person like me is supposed to be interested in. Indeed, one of the great things about really getting to know the *Twilight* series, from my perspective, is that it breaks down a barrier that's supposed to exist between me and its broader audience.

When I'm teaching a class and I need an example of a movie that my 18- and 19-year-old students will be familiar with, *Twilight* is there for me. When I'm at a large family gathering trying to make conversation with my cousin's 14-year-old daughter who I haven't seen in five years, *Twilight* is there for me. But here's the worry: if my young relative loves *Twilight* because she thinks it's straightforwardly good, whereas I love it partly because it's bad, am I implicitly making fun of her when we dish about how much more we like Edward than Jacob? I hope not.

I'll attempt to sort all this out in the rest of this chapter.

***

We experience the formation of our taste as a process guided primarily by passive responses. We try out lots of stuff and find ourselves liking some things and disliking others. We follow the strands that appeal to us and abandon the ones that don't. If I really love a Sergio Leone movie, I might turn around and watch his other movies. If I like those, I might seek out titles by other directors who are reputed to have similar qualities, and start working through the films of Sergio Corbucci and Sergio Sollima. If I like these, I might branch out beyond the first name "Sergio" and hunt for increasingly obscure Italian westerns and crime films from the era. I might thereby develop a taste for Italian genre films of the 1960s and 70s without ever having had the goal of doing so. I simply followed the lead of my own passive responses.

But what if the responses that guide this process aren't as passive as they seem? For one thing, the attitudes and expectations that we approach an artwork with can have a big impact on how we experience it. I think of myself as someone who loves the films of Dario Argento and dislikes the films of Luca Guadagnino. When I watched Argento's *Dracula 3D*, I was primed to enjoy it. I approached it with a generous attitude. Where others saw a shoddy production, I saw a delightful homage to the Dracula films that were produced from the 1950s through the 70s by the British studio Hammer. When I watched Guadagnino's 2018 remake of Argento's towering classic *Suspiria*, in contrast, I was armed with my harshest, most critical attitude. Argento himself said of the remake: "It did not excite me, it betrayed the spirit of the original film: there is no fear, there is no music." I believed him, and so I approached it actively looking for flaws that would affirm my expectation that it was going to be bad. It was easy to find them. I was open to the possibility that adding extended dance choreography would be an interesting way to update *Suspiria*, but as soon as I saw that the garish editing makes it impossible to follow the choreography, the movie had no chance with me. All I could focus on from that point forward were more things to dislike about it: the godawful Thom Yorke score, the drab color scheme, the bad digital effects, the bastardization of the mythology of Argento's Three Mothers Trilogy, and so on. It's not that I am *pretending* to like *Dracula 3D* and dislike the *Suspiria* remake—my responses are sincere. It's rather that whether I like these films or not depends in part on my approach to engaging with them, which, in turn, depends in part on how I want to think of my taste. I'm an Argento fan. I embrace that (and all that it entails) as part of who I am. But don't mistake me for a guy who likes the *Suspiria* remake.

In his influential book *Distinction: A Social Critique of the Judgment of Taste*, French philosopher and sociologist Pierre Bourdieu develops the theory that taste functions primarily as a way for the upper classes of society to distinguish themselves from the lower classes. This is an oversimplification, but for illustrative purposes we might say that the middle class gravitates towards Oscar-winning films as a way to distinguish itself as educated and refined and therefore unlike the lower class that revels in violent action movies and raunchy sex comedies. Meanwhile, the upper class distinguishes itself from the middle class by rejecting popular media altogether and dressing up in tuxedos and evening gowns to see the latest staging of *Tristan und Isolde* at the opera house.

Bourdieu famously wrote: "Tastes are perhaps first and foremost distastes, disgusts provoked by horror or visceral intolerance of the tastes of others."[2] Characteristically, members of the middle class don't merely prefer Oscar-grubbing prestige dramas to violent action movies, they are appalled by the degenerate taste of an audience with the opposite preference and they relish the sense of superiority they feel on account of this difference. Members of the upper class are similarly appalled at the middle class's naïve idea of what elevated culture looks like and feel similarly superior when they have the opportunity to declare that they don't watch television or pay attention to new movies, but that they are eagerly awaiting the upcoming Japanese sculpture exhibit at the museum.

Bourdieu's ideas about taste are powerful and illuminating, but his emphasis on class renders his account overly narrow. We use taste to distinguish ourselves from others in many ways, not just along class boundaries. Music critic Carl Wilson offers a helpful example to illustrate the broader applications of Bourdieu's concept of distinction:

> The clearest way to understand distinction may be in high-school terms: Say you're a white, nerdy fifteen-year-old boy who listens to *High School Musical* (if you're too old to know what *High School Musical* is, substitute the Andrew Lloyd Webber of your choice) but you come to see you have a chance of becoming friends with the tough kids who smoke behind the school. So you start listening to death metal and wearing hacked-up jean jackets. This isn't a ruse: you just start to see what's *plausible* and *exciting* for you about those tastes ... Your instinct is to distinguish yourself from the nerds by becoming one of the tough kids, who, incidentally, hate *High School Musical* (or *Cats*) with a vengeance because that's what nerds listen to. That's distinction.[3]

Taste is a way to associate ourselves with people with whom we want to be associated and distance ourselves from people from whom we want to be distanced. Wilson develops a variant of Bourdieu's theory of distinction in his 2007 book *Let's Talk About Love: A Journey to the End of Taste*. The book is about Celine Dion, who was at once spectacularly popular and critically reviled in the late 1990s and early 2000s. Wilson asks how it could be that the work of an artist whom critics find so contemptible resonates so strongly with so many people. When we consider Bourdieu's concept of distinction, an explanation suggests itself: critics and the rest of the self-styled cultural elite distinguish themselves as superior precisely by rejecting the tastes of the naïve masses. This is not to say that they *pretend* to dislike Celine Dion in order to create the appearance of distinction;

their dislike is genuine, but it is shaped and amplified by her popularity and the condescending sense that her fans just don't know enough to see what's wrong with her music.

Over the course of his exploration, Wilson comes to realize that, while Celine Dion will never be his favorite, there is a lot more to her music and the way her fans appreciate it than the cultural elite acknowledge. He discovers, for instance, that her singing in French (her native language) is more emotionally dynamic and nuanced than her singing in English—a difference that he could only pick up on once he set aside his prejudices and cultivated an open and generous attitude. He also discovers that Celine Dion's music is deeply meaningful to a lot of likable people who don't deserve sneering disdain.

Twilight is my Celine Dion. At one point, I thought I was too cool for it, but it turns out that I'm less cool than I thought. The joy I get out of embracing *Twilight* is much more satisfying than the sense of superiority I once got from rejecting it. Getting over oneself is a beautiful thing.

Much like Celine Dion, beating up on the *Twilight* movies is a favorite pastime of critics and self-styled cultural elites. To be fair, there are a wide range of opinions out there, and some prominent commentators have offered full-throated defenses, but perusing reviews reveals a preponderance of dismissive takes, especially for the sequels. As I've already discussed, one very common line of criticism is that it's "for girls." Here are a couple examples from critics included in the Rotten Tomatoes aggregate:

> Steve Newton: Stephenie Meyer's series of four romantic vampire novels—of which 2005's *Twilight* was the first—have proven incredibly popular among teens. But unless you're a 14-year-old girl who gets all giddy at the

thought of cute boys and first love, steer clear of *Thirteen* director Catherine Hardwicke's anemic adaptation.[4]

Frank Ochieng: Twilight sparkles for its intended audience of indiscriminate adolescent females. However, it will only be deemed as a softened, hackneyed horror show of synthetic affection for the rest of us.[5]

And here's an example of a Rotten Tomatoes user review, from Logan W.:

> Awful all-around. Granted I'm not the target demographic for these movies, it can't be salvaged that these movies have no production value and are a total cash-grab. God get this shoddily-produced crap outta my face. This spawned a whole crap cavalry of movies. It created a mush-gush genre of sucky vampire shows and movies. The epidemic of raging teenage hormones driving girls to drinking over Team Edward or Team Jacob. Like who the hell cares. They literally claw each other's eyes out, bite each other's heads off just to get a closer shot of Taylor Lautner's abs. They're basically screaming "take my money."

These three takes don't merely take note of the fact that the intended audience of *Twilight* is adolescent girls; they insinuate that the film is bad *because* they are its intended audience. The contempt on display is revealing. There is a long legacy of "women's pictures" and "chick flicks" that men make a big show of not wanting to watch except as a grand concession for Valentine's Day or their spouse's birthday. Critics dislike *Twilight* for a variety of reasons, but the extra-special contempt that it attracts in reviews like the ones quoted above has something to do with its gender associations. I propose that these associations present a valuable opportunity: for some demographics, embracing *Twilight* can be a way of resisting gender expectations. It's not unlike the phenomenon of the "Brony"—the adult male fan of *My Little Pony: Friendship is Magic*. Bronyism rejects the cultural coding of *My Little Pony* as being for young girls and also the pernicious norms restricting the range of things that men are supposed to like. Bronies aren't making fun of *My Little Pony*, they love it and they spread its gospel. There are a number of proud celebrity Bronies out there, including Andrew W. K., Chris Evans, and William Shatner (who tweeted "Friendship is Magic!" when the topic came up). The popularity of Bronyism creates a path for adult men to resist gender norms by embracing a delightful, uplifting cartoon. But there are also many other opportunities to do this, and *Twilight* is one of them.

One might immediately worry: "But wait, if you like it because it's bad, doesn't that just reinforce exactly the sort of gendered contempt you're talking about?" This is a tricky point, and one that I will address at length in the second half of this chapter, but the short answer is that one needs to keep in mind what I mean by "bad." A movie is bad in the relevant sense if it violates received norms in a way that is not perceived as artistically serious. When I say that I like *Twilight* in part because it's bad, I don't mean that in a negative way. I mean that I like it in part because of the ways it disrupts the expectations that we bring to the movies with us.

One thing I value about popular film in general is the way that it gives people who don't have much in common something to talk about. For any random person I meet, it's unlikely that we've read many of the same books and we probably don't listen to the same music, but we've almost certainly seen a lot of the same movies. A beautiful aspect of Bad Movie Love,

I want to suggest, is the way it can so readily cut across ordinary social barriers. If we can use taste to distinguish ourselves from other people, we can also use it to break down such distinctions.

But then why not just go all in on all the most popular movies? Back in Chapter 1, I worried that offerings at the multiplex are becoming too homogenous. Perhaps the considerations I've brought up in this chapter suggest that homogenization is something to celebrate. If most people like the same thing, doesn't that do a lot to break down barriers and build connections between people from different walks of life?

I don't think so. If we all liked the same movies, this commonality between us would just be a background fact that we would take for granted in much the same way that we take for granted that most everyone likes a glass of cool water on a hot day. A world in which we all liked the same things would be dull and colorless. While we would have a lot in common, our conversations would quickly become repetitive. "Seen any good movies lately?" "Same ones as you!" While I do value the way that *Twilight* breaks down barriers between me and a lot of people I otherwise don't have much in common with, it wouldn't work that way if *everyone* liked *Twilight*. In that case, meeting a fellow *Twilight* fan would barely be worth a shrug. Just think about how deeply unexciting it is to discover that someone likes The Beatles.

In his book *On Being Awesome: A Unified Theory of How Not to Suck*, philosopher Nick Riggle writes: "Being awesome is a matter of creatively breaking out of, or riffing on, norms that determine much of everyday life, and doing so in an expressive way, generating a social opening that allows for the mutual appreciation of individuality."[6] Bad Movie Love is awesome, in Riggle's sense; it steps outside the scripts generated by received norms and creates social openings that allow for the mutual appreciation of individuality. Although I do love staying up late by myself to watch bad movies, the enterprise is especially well-suited to social gatherings. Bad movies bring people together and promote communal experiences. Especially during exploratory bad movie viewing ("Wanna come over and watch the new DTV John Travolta movie? It could be a waste of time but there's also a chance it will be amazing"), it often happens that one person will notice something funny or bizarre or otherwise interesting about a movie that others miss. Sharing these idiosyncratic observations and influencing one another's experience of the movie adds a social dimension to aesthetic engagement that affords participants an opportunity for the mutual appreciation of individuality. Coming together to find unconventional ways of appreciating a movie that has been neglected or disdained also helps us find unconventional ways of appreciating each other. Ridicule might also accomplish this, but in the non-awesome mode of condescension. I submit that it is more socially satisfying to collaboratively discover neglected treasures than it is to tear something down because it's weird and different.

For an analysis of the social implications of Bad Movie Love, it will be helpful to consider philosopher Ted Cohen's theory of jokes. Cohen thinks that jokes depend on a shared context between the teller of the joke and the audience. A Jewish person himself, he offers a range of examples of jokes about Judaisim and Jewish people that depend on shared familiarity with certain aspects of Jewish culture. Because jokes depend on this sort of shared context, they create a sense of *intimacy*. Cohen writes:

> And just what is this *intimacy*? It is the shared sense of those in a *community*. The members know that they are in this community, and they know that they are joined there by

> one another. When the community is focused on a joke, the intimacy has two constituents. The first constituent is a shared set of beliefs, dispositions, prejudices, preferences, et cetera—a shared outlook on the world, or at least part of an outlook. The second constituent is a shared feeling—a shared response to something. The first constituent can be cultivated and realized without jokes. So can the second constituent, but with jokes, the second constituent is amplified by the first, and this is a very curious and wonderful fact about jokes.[7]

The shared context that jokes rely on amplifies our shared responses and the sense of intimacy they create. When we laugh together at a joke that many would lack the context to understand, our mutual recognition that we both "get it" can make the joke funnier to us and at the same time foster a satisfying feeling of connection. The clearest examples of this are "private jokes" between close friends or couples. A couple might have a running joke about how one of them sounds like a donkey when they snore, and they might burst out laughing at a dinner party when no one else does because someone brought up the topic of donkeys. Experiences like this can make a couple feel closer to one another. This kind of private joke depends on the intimacy of a romantic relationship or close friendship, but it can also enhance such intimacy. Idiosyncratic engagement with bad movies can work the same way. When I watch bad movies with my buddy Jesse, we laugh not only because the movies are funny, but also because we appreciate one another's sensibilities. We've watched dozens of movies together that have a giant "supercomputer" prop that's obviously built out of cardboard, and now we laugh every time we hear the "bleep bleep bloop bloop" sound effects that are always used when someone presses a button. Most people would not laugh at these moments; our shared amusement is a sort of private joke. This social dimension of our engagement with bad movies enhances both our enjoyment of the movies and our friendship.

In his essay "High and low thinking about high and low art," Ted Cohen applies this idea to larger groups that coalesce around appreciating works of art. He introduces the concept of an *affective community*, "a group whose intimacy is underwritten by their conviction that they feel the same about something, and that that thing—the art—is their bond. They feel that one another respond in the same way, and for the same reasons."[8] Consider the scene at a concert before the band starts playing. Nearly everyone in attendance has at least one thing in common: they like the band. This creates a context where it becomes socially appropriate to walk up to a stranger, offer a high five, and say "are you pumped or what, my dude?!" An implicit bond exists between everyone at the show, and this bond is based on their mutual recognition that they have similar feelings about the music.

This dynamic extends to Bad Movie Lovers. If I'm hanging out with a mixed group of people I don't know very well, but everyone present is a fan of *The Room*, I can promote a sense of intimacy by sharing my personal perspective about what's so wonderful about *The Room*. Most people wouldn't get it, and the fact that this group appreciates what I'm saying creates a feeling of connectedness. We all like this same weird thing; our *Room* fandom is idiosyncratic, but also shared. Bad movies are exciting in part because they forge unlikely connections between people from different walks of life. They give us a path to break free from restrictive norms and practice creative forms of engagement that generate opportunities for valuable social interactions involving the mutual appreciation of individuality.

But when too many people are connected by a shared context, this effect is diluted. There's a saying that "a friend to all is a friend to none." The more people we are connected to in a given way, the less significant each individual connection is. If one corporation ruled movie theaters and our collective taste conformed to their products, we would have *too much* in common. When an affective community gets too large, the feelings of connectedness it grounds are weakened. I don't get excited to meet someone who enjoys the original Star Wars trilogy, but it is absolutely thrilling to meet another 40-year-old man who appreciates *Twilight*. Sure, *Twilight* is very popular in its own right, but not with people like me. When my students find out that I know the *Twilight* movies extremely well they are far more excited than they are when they learn that I—like everyone else—enjoy *The Empire Strikes Back*.

***

But now, the rub: what if I meet someone who loves *Twilight* and thinks it is superlatively great in a totally straightforward way—call this person Twilight Tammy—while I think that it's good-bad? Am I condescending to Tammy when we gab about *Twilight*? Am I implicitly making fun of her? I hope not.

Ted Cohen's initial account of affective communities implies that fans of a work of art constitute an intimate group because of their mutual recognition that they respond to a work of art in the same way. In the case I've just described, however, we *don't* respond in the same way. When Edward says to Bella: "Your scent is like a drug to me. You're my own personal brand of heroin," I laugh hysterically. Twilight Tammy does not laugh, she swoons. She finds this line romantic; I find it absurd. Are we part of the same affective community?

Cohen raises this issue in his piece, "High and low art, and high and low audiences":

> My late father and I both greatly enjoyed a number of John Wayne movies, especially those directed by John Ford and Howard Hawks. But as I grew older it began to seem to me that my father and I responded to different things in those movies, and indeed we sometimes barely recognized one another's descriptions of the same movies. When you love a work of art, you are likely to want others to care for it as well. Does it matter to you whether they like it for the same reasons as you?[9]

The fact that Ted Cohen and his father responded to John Wayne movies in very different ways did not prevent the two of them from enjoying the time they spent together watching them. Suppose they watch Howard Hawks' *Hatari!* together and Cohen sees it as a sophisticated examination of the way that masculinity is constructed in opposition to the concept of civilization while his father sees it as a rollicking adventure about some guys who capture giraffes and rhinos. Would anyone think that Cohen is implicitly making fun of his father's simplistic way of looking at the film? I hope not! Cohen was presumably very glad to have something to bond with his father over, and it surely did not diminish the value of their shared activity to discover that they didn't respond in exactly the same way. Indeed, Cohen may have valued—without condescension—his father's uncomplicated and joyous way of relating to the movie. I know that when I watched movies with my aging father the last thing on my mind was how simplistic his interpretations were.

I was just happy that we had the chance to enjoy something together. I hope that Twilight Tammy and I can find the same sort of common ground, but I must acknowledge that *Twilight* is a trickier case than *Hatari!*. Special hazards arise in cases where one person loves a movie because it's so bad it's good while the other rejects the suggestion that it's bad.

These hazards are much greater for the derisive *Mystery Science Theater* 3000 approach to engaging with bad movies. Unfortunately, the practice of ridiculing bad movies for fun is very prominent, and this creates the impression that Bad Movie Love is all about heckling bad movies. It's not! As I've discussed, Ridicule is a distinct practice where movies are used as prompts for improvisational comedy. I personally have never been able to enjoy *MST3K* or *RiffTrax*. I want the hecklers to shut up so I can enjoy the movie. Bad Movie Love is a higher path, and one that can potentially enable me to bond with Twilight Tammy in a sincere way.

My love of *Twilight* is multifaceted. As I explained above, I think that the series has straightforward artistic merits. The portrayal of anxious, frightened lust in the first movie is interesting in much the same way that an art film with similar subject matter might be. *Breaking Dawn – Part 1* is excellent pregnancy horror and I like it in much the same way that I might like an indie pregnancy horror movie with more street cred. But a big part of what I love about the series is the variety of ways in which it transgresses received norms. I wouldn't have been able to get to the point where I appreciate other aspects of the movies if I hadn't first embraced them as good-bad.

One thing I enjoy about the series is the way that throughout *New Moon* and *Eclipse* Jacob never misses a chance to take off his shirt. When Bella crashes a motorcycle and her scalp is bleeding, Jacob doesn't hesitate to take off his shirt and use it to daintily dab her wound. It's raining out and he's in a hurry? Off comes the shirt as he breaks into a sprint. It would be hard to overstate how many times he takes off his shirt. I love these moments; they crack me up. Twilight Tammy likes them as well, but it's because she gets to see Taylor Lautner's sexy abs. My laughter is not mean-spirited. I'm not cracking jokes about dumb it is that the guy can't keep his shirt on. I'm not making fun of the notion that someone would enjoy ogling Lautner's taut physique. I'm laughing because the shameless excess of scenes where Jacob takes his shirt off is in such stark contrast to received norms about male nudity in popular films. We are accustomed to gratuitous female nudity in movies (especially those of us who grew up in the 1980s), but man flesh is usually either presented alongside female nudity or in hypermasculine contexts like a shirtless Sylvester Stallone mowing down communists with a machine gun. Lautner's incessant shirtlessness in *New Moon* and *Eclipse* stands out because there is no reason for it other than the titillation of the audience.

The difference between my reaction and Tammy's is grounded in the fact that we are not in the grip of the same set of norms. From where I'm sitting, Jacob's shirtlessness is funny because it's so obtrusively gratuitous. Tammy, unlike me, did not grow up in the 1980s. The *Twilight* movies were among the first films she ever became interested in, and so she's not in the grip of the norms that I experience the movie as transgressing. It need not be the case that I'm at any level making fun of her when we enjoy watching and discussing *Twilight* together. I'm not laughing at the movie out of a sense of superiority or self-satisfied disdain, I genuinely admire it. It's just that I admire it from a different frame of reference. Suppose that Tammy is a niece I don't get to see very often and I'm interested in getting to know her better. We might bond over the *Twilight* series in a way that is meaningful to both of us, even though we respond to the movies in different ways. Ted Cohen asks: "When you love a work of art, you are likely to want others to care for it as well. Does it matter to you whether they like it for the same reasons as you?"[10] In a case like the one I've described, surely what matters most is the opportunity to bond with my niece. The difference between our responses is far less important than the fact that we enjoy the movie together.

And it's important not to overstate the difference in our responses. We would both laugh when Bella angrily berates Jacob in *Breaking Dawn – Part 2*: "You nicknamed my daughter after the Loch Ness Monster?!!!" We would both groan with annoyance at Edward's nonsensical pretext for being absent for nearly the entirety of *New Moon*. We would both grin at Michael Sheen chewing scenery as Aro, leader of the Volturi. If our responses sharply diverge at some points, it is my responsibility to be conscientious about how she might experience the interaction. If I laugh a little too hard in a romantic scene and I get the sense that Tammy feels like I'm making fun of her sincere emotional investment, I need to adjust my tone in order for the interaction to be positive for both of us. If it's hard to read her reactions, I should err on the side of caution.

Bad Movie Love promotes these sorts of interaction across ordinary social boundaries. To be clear, non-bad movies can also play this role, but bad movies are particularly apt. Bad Movie Love is about breaking free from the narrowness of received norms, and so it naturally tends to lead us to contexts that are unusual for us. The entire genre of DTV martial arts movies is transgressive relative to some contexts, but it is an utterly normal thing to be interested in for the Mixed

Martial Arts (MMA) community. As I discussed in Chapter 3, I'm interested in DTV action movies partly because of the way many of them focus on bodies in motion rather than character and narrative. The way these movies transgress received norms is part of what interests me about them. But MMA fans are not as likely to be in the grips of these norms. They are practiced at watching martial arts competitions and so it's easy for them to focus on the action for its own sake. They don't need character and narrative to hook their interest. Although I may not otherwise have much in common with any given MMA fan, we can have an absolutely delightful conversation about the two dozen Scott Adkins movies we've both seen.

The internet massively expands the scale of opportunity for this sort of interaction. Many Facebook groups function as online clubhouses for affective communities built around various sorts of good-bad, cult, and genre movies. Here are some examples of Facebook groups that I am a member of:

Cannon Films Appreciation Society
Movies "So Bad They're Good," Midnight Cult Classics, and Camp
The Grind: Grindhouse, Exploitation and Underground Cinema 18+
SCOTT ADKINS OFFICIAL FANS
DOLPH LUNDGREN FAN CLUB

For the most part, I have almost nothing in common with the people I interact with in these groups aside from our shared love of the Cannon Group, good-bad movies, exploitation sleaze, Scott Adkins, and/or Dolph Lundgren. Even during this extra shitty era of global politics, in which everyone is wallowing in dire hatred of everyone else, people who like the

Cannon Group enough to join the Cannon Films Appreciation Society can more or less get along. In this narrow context, no one knows or cares what anyone else's political orientation is. We can leave our differences at the door and slap five over our common love of *Over the Top* and *Revenge of the Ninja*.

My brother Josh and I are huge fans of Charles Bronson, who starred in eight Cannon Group films in the 1980s. When Josh's son was born last year, he and his wife Isabel went right ahead and named the little guy Charles Bronson Strohl. Reader, I was giddy—both about the nephew and the name. I realize, however, that not everyone is in a position to appreciate how completely and utterly badass a christening this was. I can totally imagine some goober rolling their eyes at the announcement. I wanted a safe space to bask in joy over the news, so I posted a picture on the Cannon Films Appreciation Society page of little Charley in a Charles Bronson onesie I had bought him. I got a warm and celebratory response from strangers all over the world. Many people posted congratulatory Charles Bronson memes; one guy shared that he had named his own son Bronson. That guy definitely gets it! This interaction created a sense of intimacy between me and these strangers over our shared love for Charles Bronson and our mutual recognition that it is extremely awesome to be named after him.

Philosophers Sam Cowling and Wesley D. Cray draw a similar connection between systematic engagement with junk comic books and Ted Cohen's notion of affective communities. They write:

> Junk comics bind together communities—fandoms—and while these communities can certainly be toxic in many ways (see, for example, ComicsGate, GamerGate, the Sad

> Puppies, and unfortunately, others) they can also offer a profound sense of belonging and shared interest, shared agency, and shared humanity. Batman fandom needn't be a game of solitaire: it can be a valuable, intimate, and multifaceted group activity. Insofar as junk comics facilitate such an activity, we have at least some reason to not just engage with them, but celebrate them. You need not—and probably ought not—devote your entire life to reading junk comics, but, at the same time, you need not suffer any kind of aesthetic or philosophical embarrassment in making room for them.[11]

When I proudly posted a picture of my newborn nephew in the Cannon Films Appreciation Society Facebook page and got exactly the kind of enthusiastic response I was hoping for, I experienced the sense of belonging and shared interest that Cowling and Cray are talking about. Over time, participation in affective communities can lead to the formation of personal friendships based on common interests. Some of the people I spend the most time talking about movies with are people who I've never met in person. An interest in movies can serve as the basis for valuable social relationships, and these relationships can in turn enhance our engagement with movies.

***

Bad Movie Love can bring people together across ordinary social barriers. Engaging with bad movies in the mode of Ridicule tends to work in the opposite direction. If my hobby is to invite my friends with humanities PhDs over to sip cocktails and haughtily make fun of *Twilight*'s inadequacies, that's not going to put me in a position to have a positive interaction with Twilight Tammy and it's not going to make me feel like Tammy and I are part of the same affective community. If I watch Cannon Group films to make fun of the writing and acting, that isn't going to lead to rewarding interactions with the affective community that loves Cannon and it's not going to lead to a round of high fives over the birth of little Charles Bronson. Ridicule is all about reinforcing divisions. Making fun of *Twilight* or Cannon is a way of basking in what Bourdieu called "distinction": the sense that our taste makes us *better* than the artists whose work we think is bad and the audiences whose taste we disdain. Can you form a community around Ridicule? Sure, such communities are commonplace. But what sort of communities are they? I could see how someone who is interested in improvisational comedy could get a lot of value out of being involved, but a movie lover? As I've emphasized, Ridicule is a backhanded way of enforcing received norms. It bolsters the sense that there's something wrong with liking these movies and that the only way to enjoy them is to talk over them. It's a deeply conformist way of relating to the medium. Every now and then someone wanders into one of the Facebook groups mentioned above and starts spouting mockery, and it's like they pooped in the punchbowl. Here we all are, slapping five about how much we love the Charles Bronson sleazefest *10 to Midnight*, and some jerk rolls in with a bullshit tone of mocking superiority. The group is all about celebrating the oddball charms of Cannon. Looking down on the movies is not a way of doing that.

One might object that I am misconstruing the nature of Ridicule, and that it's not as mean-spirited as I make it out to be. One might think of the sort of heckling found in MST3K and *RiffTrax* as another form of affectionate engagement involving a rhetorical game of pretending to be mean. I don't buy that for a minute. I've seen this stuff myself. It's harsh and condescending. The hecklers are lazy and smug. If they're pretending to be mean, they're extremely good at pretending. MST3K at least has a fictional world of its own that provides some mitigating context, but its descendant *RiffTrax* and the majority of their copycats have nothing to offer but derision. I find it profoundly unfunny. I hate it deep in my bones. Keep that shit away from me.

One might further object that MST3K, *RiffTrax*, and the glut of bad movie podcasts and YouTube channels focused on Ridicule at least play the positive role of bringing income and attention to the artists behind the movies. There is, after all, no such thing as bad publicity. As publicity goes, Ridicule might be effective, but that doesn't make it any less distasteful. It may be an economic reality that many artists have benefited from their works being ridiculed, but that's a sad reality. Wikipedia lists a number of examples of artists being outraged and offended by the way MST3K handled their films.[12] Japanese studio Kadokawa Pictures refused to allow an American distributor to release their Gamera films because they were so angered by the way MST3K had mocked them. They chose dignity over the monetary benefits of this sort of publicity, and the films were not released in North America until Kadokawa no longer controlled the rights.

Of course, artists don't (and shouldn't) get to decide how their work is received, but I bring up these examples to illustrate why I don't believe that Ridicule is just another form of Love. Hecklers are not interested in trying to understand what might be interesting or appealing about these movies in the way that Bad Movie Lovers are. I'm sure that Ridicule is fun for many people, but it is not something I would ever want to be a part of, and I hereby submit (with my John Lennon glasses on) that Love is a higher path.

Nicolas Cage and the Limits of the Critical Imagination

Five

In the bargain basement DTV noir *Grand Isle*, which sits at 0% on the Tomatometer, Nicolas Cage plays a former Marine living in Louisiana with his wife, Fancy. After damaging his fence in the process of shooting an intruder, he hires a strapping young sailor named Buddy to repair it. While Buddy is hard at work in the blazing heat with sweat glistening on his muscles, Fancy seductively sashays out and offers him some ice tea. Meanwhile, Cage gets sloshed on the porch. This is all presented as a flashback from a later point when Buddy is being questioned by a Bible-thumping detective with a robust Foghorn Leghorn accent, played by Kelsey Grammer. The detective suspects him of murder, but we don't yet know who he is supposed to have killed. When Buddy asks for a lawyer and a phone call, Grammer forcefully retorts: "What you think this is, New York? D.C.? You're in GRAND ISLE, son. We don't subscribe to that big city nonsense."

I started to wonder at this point if the story was going to turn out to be that Fancy had seduced Buddy and put him up to murdering her husband, which would be a very standard direction for a movie like this to go. To say that I was surprised by where it ended up going instead would be a vast understatement. *Grand Isle* is 100% certified bonkers. It takes a hard left turn when Buddy is stuck overnight by the combination of car

DOI: 10.4324/9780367808969-5

trouble and a hurricane, and Cage—with a patchy Louisiana accent—strikes up this exchange at the dinner table:

Cage: "You know about deception, don't you?"
Buddy: "Not sure I follow."
Cage: "I mean, I can tell you're having problems at home. An example, um, when was the last time you had your, uh, COCK, um, SUCKED?"
Buddy: "Excuse me?"
Cage: "That long, huh? Egad. You know what else I can tell?"
Buddy: "What's that?"
Cage: "I can tell you wanna fuck my wife."

I won't spoil it here, but the narrative is a sort of Frankenstein monster, cramming two movies worth of twists into its 97 minute running time. *Grand Isle* is a stew of pulpy southern noir, boiled down till it makes no sense. And it's dedicated to the troops! It's exactly the kind of Nicolas Cage movie that I most look forward to. There's not much of a budget and relatively little at stake, which gives everyone involved the freedom to get weird to an extent that is just barely commercially viable. It's a movie I would recommend to almost no one, but that I will occasionally rewatch for the rest of my life.

I'm a Nicolas Cage fan. As I write this, I've seen 88 Nicolas Cage movies, most of them more than once. When a new Cage title comes out, I watch it as soon as I can get my hands on it. I don't care if it's at 4% or 98% on the Tomatometer—just give it to me; I want it. When *Grand Isle* was released to no fanfare whatsoever, I was ready with my $5.99 to rent and watch it that night, by myself, at midnight. I was enraptured. I periodically mumbled things to myself like "now *this* is what I'm talking about" and "oh yeah, that's the good stuff."

Cage has seen a resurgence in popularity in recent years, but this resurgence hasn't translated into attention for projects like *Grand Isle*. This does not in any way surprise me, but I was still irked to read the handful of contemptuous reviews published on the film, especially when I got to this quote from Gary M. Kramer, writing for Salon:

> And one might think Cage playing a Vietnam Vet with a drinking problem—as he does here—would generate some of his beloved manic scenery chewing. But director Stephen S. Campanelli, never allows Cage to quite go as batshit crazy as his fans want.[1]

Speaking as a Cage fan, I beg to differ. We all know the meme version of Nicolas Cage. He screams, he yells, he makes faces: it's very memeable. This critic's mistake is conflating the Cage-as-meme phenomenon with his cult of fandom. Cage has a lot more to offer than going "batshit crazy." There are many varieties of Nicolas Cage. Indeed, there is a *galaxy* of Nicolas Cage, and his fans find something to love about pretty much all of it. There are maybe five Cage performances I shrug at and *Grand Isle* is sure as hell not one of them. His performance doesn't involve a lot of high volume hysterics, but it is full of drunken swagger, weird ticks, and dark humor. Several times in the movie, he just stares off into space and blinks repeatedly in an exaggerated way. He's playing that he's so drunk the room is spinning and he's trying to regain his equilibrium. I almost always find Cage captivating to watch in part because he weaves so many details like this into his performances.

I understand why professional critics with jobs at major publications do not like *Grand Isle*. It is a bad movie. It stomps all over received norms. What's striking about this review is the way Kramer predicts that *Nicolas Cage fans* will dislike it. It's one thing to say that most people wouldn't like it, but he's talking about *fans*. His prediction presumes a penetrating understanding of what it is that Cage's fans like about his work. Alas, he lacks such an understanding.

Kramer's mistake is rooted in a failure of imagination. He is unable to envision how a Nicolas Cage fan might view the movie. His own familiarity with Cage cultism is limited to the meme version, and since there aren't a lot of GIF-worthy moments in *Grand Isle*, he can't see how a committed Cage aficionado might find value in it. He doesn't even know what to look for.

In this chapter, I want to consider the career of Nicolas Cage and its critical reception in some depth. I intend this primarily as film criticism: I'm here to make the case for my guy. But there's also some philosophy in the background. We'll consider in this chapter the way that received norms and popular perceptions can act as a limiting horizon for the critical imagination.

We'll also return to the idea, introduced in Chapter 1, that the boundary between the good-bad and the avant-garde is often drawn arbitrarily, and that movies that are initially received as bad are often rehabilitated down the road. Bad Movie Lovers sometimes act as a critical vanguard, upending critical assumptions and charting new ways of engaging with movies, some of which are later embraced by the mainstream. With Nicolas Cage, we can see this process happening in real time, as he is currently seeing a resurgence of popularity and critical respectability.

Cage's acting career can be roughly divided into four overlapping divisions, listed here along with representative examples:

Early period: *Peggy Sue Got Married*, *Vampire's Kiss*
Movie star period: *Face/Off*, *The Rock*
DTV period: *The Trust*, *Army of One*
Comeback: *Mandy*, *Color Out of Space*

There is a dominant narrative—often taken for granted by mainstream critics—according to which Cage peaked as an artist somewhere in the overlap between the Early period and Movie star period and then fell off and did lousy work in the DTV period before being made palatable for mainstream consumption again through the viral celebration of his persona. I will argue that we should reject this narrative, but first we need to understand its basis.

Huddle around, everyone, it's time for a Nicolas Cage history lesson.

***

Thanks in part to the fact that he's the nephew of legendary director Francis Ford Coppola, he was cast in is his first movie (*Fast Times at Ridgemont High*) at the age of 17. Wanting to be judged on his own merits rather than his family legacy, he changed his last name from Coppola to Cage and started looking for work. He was picked out of a pile of headshots by director Martha Coolidge and cast in her 1983 romantic comedy *Valley Girl*. He plays a Hollywood punk who becomes Romeo to a privileged Juliet from the San Fernando Valley. His performance is magnetic. It's full of erratic energy, dynamic inflection, frenetic gesticulation, and huge emotion. He makes a big impression. His career was anything but a slow starter.

Two of his most significant early performances were his roles in Alan Parker's *Birdy* and Francis Ford Coppola's *Peggy Sue Got Married*. *Birdy* was a critical success and Cage's performance was widely praised. The film tells the story of a pair of friends, played by Cage and Matthew Modine, and it alternates between two timelines, one set during their high school days and the other set years later as they struggle with physical and psychological trauma after returning from the Vietnam War. The two main characters are an odd couple: Cage is a high school Casanova and star athlete; Modine is an asexual introvert who's obsessed with birds. The earlier timeline recounts the story of their friendship in a loose, episodic style that lets us really spend some time getting to know them. I find this section of the movie unusually beautiful. The oversexed high school alpha male is a perennial 1980s movie villain, but, in *Birdy*, Cage turns this cliché on its head and give us an oversexed high school alpha male who deeply loves the most unpopular guy in school. In the later timeline, Cage's character's face has been severely wounded in combat. He needed dental work around the time they started filming, so as preparation for the role he had two teeth extracted without anesthetic and then wore his bandages around the set at all times. This section of the movie is *heavy*, and Cage and Modine lay it all out. The film alternates between the visceral pain of this post-Vietnam timeline and the berserk comic energy of the high school timeline, and the wild shifts in tone are exhilarating.

Cage's performance in *Peggy Sue Got Married* is a complete departure from *Birdy*. Coppola's romantic comedy depicts a jaded Kathleen Turner who is in the process of divorcing her cheating husband (Cage) when she has a heart arrhythmia at her 25th high school reunion, passes out, and travels back in time to her teenage years. She has the chance to make different decisions and avoid marrying Cage's character in the first place. Coppola wanted his nephew to be in the movie (he also cast his daughter, Sofia, as Peggy Sue's sister), but Cage didn't want to do it. He eventually signed on, but only under the condition that he could do something really far out. Because most of the movie takes place in Peggy Sue's dream, and because dreams are often strange and distorted, he thought it would be the perfect opportunity to experiment with surrealistic acting.[2] Specifically, he wanted to talk like Pokey, the horse from *The Gumby Show*. And talk like Pokey he does! His performance comes across as especially strange because he is the only cast member who took his role in a weird direction. Everyone else plays it straight. In a 2019 interview in the *New York Times*[3], he reports the reactions he got from others involved in the film: "So I went to rehearsal, and everybody was rolling their eyes because I was talking like [Pokey], and my co-star Kathleen Turner was very upset, because she wanted me to be Al, my character from *Birdy*, and instead she got Jerry Lewis on psychedelia. It did not go over well. In fact, Ray Stark from Tri-Star flew up to fire me, and thankfully Uncle went to bat and said, 'Young Nicky's doing this.' But needless to say, I never worked for them again after that."

Revisiting *Peggy Sue Got Married* many years later, it is striking that Cage was able to single-handedly turn what otherwise would have been a conventional romantic comedy into a work of surrealism. The fact that everyone else plays it straight makes the overall effect of his performance even more pronounced. Including exactly one surrealistic element in a romantic comedy is *itself* a surrealist gesture. Imagine a western that has a medieval knight as the central character, or a horror movie where the killer talks like Donald Duck (there actually is such a movie: Lucio Fulci's *The New York Ripper*). If everything else is conventional for the genre, the one surreal element has even more impact, because the conventional elements prompt us to form determinate expectations that are then crushed when someone starts talking like Pokey.

Cage's performance in *Peggy Sue Got Married* reflects a pattern that has continued throughout his career: when he takes roles that he's less excited about or signs onto more marginal projects, he finds a way to make them interesting on his own terms. I will return to this thought below when we consider Cage's DTV output, but I want to highlight that this pattern goes all the way back to the beginning of his career and is central to who he is as an artist.

One of the most remarkable aspects of Cage's early period was the way he incorporated influences into his acting that were sharply incongruous with contemporary trends. For example, he was enamored with the acting style typical of German Expressionism, which was a movement in the early 20th century characterized by the abandonment of realism in favor of surreal imagery expressing subjective experience. Expressionist films featured abstract set design and dramatic lighting reflecting the psychological condition of the characters. Silent film actors in general often used hyperbolic facial expressions and exaggerated body language to convey characters' personalities and emotions without recourse to spoken dialogue, and German Expressionism was especially extreme in this respect. The Expressionist acting style is anti-realist and characterized by bursts of violent intensity.

Cage has incorporated Expressionist elements into many of his most iconic performances. Two major examples from his early period are *Moonstruck* and *Vampire's Kiss*. In *Moonstruck*, Cage plays an opera-loving Italian American baker named Ronny who lost one of his hands in an accident he blames his brother for. Cher plays a widow who is engaged to Ronny's estranged brother. When she reaches out to invite him to the wedding, Ronny gives a fiery speech about his continuing resentment towards his brother, and, while he is ranting about losing his hand and replacing it with a prosthetic, he emulates none other than Expressionist actor Rudolf Klein-Rogge, whose character dons a mechanical hand in Fritz Lang's 1927 masterpiece *Metropolis* (image 10). Cage also wanted to speak with a guttural rasp, emulating Jean Marais in Jean Cocteau's *Beauty and The Beast*, but director Norman Jewison vetoed that plan after seeing the dailies. *Moonstruck* became a very popular film and Cage's transcendently passionate performance is one of his best-loved roles. How wonderful is it that he referenced Rudolf Klein-Rogge in a 1980s Hollywood romantic comedy and made a hit of it?

Vampire's Kiss is the single most essential Nicolas Cage movie. Penned by Joseph Minion, who also wrote Martin Scorsese's surrealist gem *After Hours*, it's the story of literary agent Peter Loew (Cage), a narcissistic yuppie with an affected Transatlantic accent who reveals in a series of therapy sessions that he may be unraveling. After one of his sexual encounters is interrupted by a bat flying through the window, he confides to his therapist that he found the subsequent struggle with the bat arousing. Not long after, he has a late night tryst with a mysterious woman, who bears a proper set of fangs and sinks them into his neck. The audience is left to wonder if this really happened or if Loew hallucinated it, as he goes on to buy a set of plastic vampire fangs and descend into the mad delusion that he himself has become a vampire.

Image 10: Metropolis (1927) (above) and *Moonstruck* (1987) (below) (*Credit: UFA and Metro-Goldwyn-Mayer*)

Cage was very excited by the project and agreed to do it for very little money (although he cost the production an extra $10k by humming a Stravinsky tune that was still under copyright). He's said many times over the years that *Vampire's Kiss* is his favorite of his own movies and that he views it as the laboratory where he developed the most distinctive elements of his acting style. After he saw the completed film, he left a message on the producer's answering machine saying it had justified his decision to become an actor. In a 2015 interview with *Time*, he explained how this role reverberated through his career:

> I was very happy with *Vampire's Kiss*, which in my opinion was almost like an independent laboratory to start realizing some of my more expressionistic dreams with film performance. Then using what I had learned in *Vampire's Kiss* and putting it into a very big action movie in the form of *Face/Off* with John Woo. If you look at those two movies back to back, you can see where I stole from my performance in *Vampire's Kiss*.[4]

Indeed, elements of Cage's *Vampire's Kiss* performance show up in *many* of his later roles, ranging from action blockbuster *Face/Off*, to his Oscar-winning performance as a suicidal alcoholic in *Leaving Las Vegas*, to his recent turn in Richard Stanley's Lovecraft adaptation *Color Out of Space*. It's the performance that most fully embodies Cage's artistic vision. There's a lot going on. He draws heavily on Expressionist influences, including Max Schrek in F. W. Murnau's *Nosferatu*, Conrad Veidt in Robert Wiene's *The Cabinet of Dr. Caligari*, and Peter Lorre in Fritz Lang's M. But it's not all so highbrow: in one scene, he eats a live cockroach. He actually ate two, as they needed a second take. During a love scene, he requested that hot yogurt be poured over his toes off camera to help him project sexual arousal. As his character's vampire delusion deepens, he executes an absolutely sublime crescendo of insanity, running down the street bellowing "I'm a vampire! I'm a vampire! I'm a vampire!"

with plastic fangs in his mouth. He characterized the style that he developed in *Vampire's Kiss* as "Nouveau Shamanic."

I'll never forget the first time I saw it. I had never heard of it before but it was available to watch and my interest in Nicolas Cage had been growing. My eyes were like saucers from start to finish. I couldn't believe what I was seeing; neither could I believe that everyone isn't talking about this movie all the time. How could something so extraordinary be so neglected?

To begin with, most early critics did not see Cage's performance as visionary, and they didn't appreciate the movie's surreal portrait of yuppiedom as psychosis. Hal Hinson wrote for the *Washington Post*:

> "Vampire's Kiss" is stone-dead bad, incoherently bad, but it goes all the way with its premise—and when I say all the way I mean all the way. You've heard of actors making a strong choice and going with it? Well, see it in the flesh! Stomping, snorting, his hair hanging over his eyes like a curtain of foppish dementia, Cage acts as if he has been taking hits off of Dennis Hopper's gas mask. There's no way to overstate it: This is scorched-earth acting—the most flagrant scenery chewing I've ever seen. Part Dwight Frye in "Dracula," part Tasmanian devil, Cage makes the previous champ—Crispin Glover in "River's Edge"—look like Perry Como. If Bierman had been able to create a compatible comic atmosphere the movie might have become an instant cult classic. And even with Cage, you have to fight your way through the uncertainties of tone, the funereal pace and the inept staging to find any enjoyment. Still, you're not exactly sure if the material is meant to be funny or is laughable merely by default.[5]

The first thing I notice in this review is Hinson's discomfort with the ambiguity of Cage's acting: is it supposed to be funny? It's so wild that one assumes so, but the events of the film are so grave that one begins to feel as though one isn't allowed to laugh. Most notably, as Peter Loew's vampire delusion progresses, he subjects his secretary to increasingly cruel forms of abuse, eventually attacking and raping her. The rape scene is intensely disturbing; it shrouds Cage's performance in a very unfunny darkness and punishes viewers who are only interested in the movie because they want to laugh at his histrionics.

Critics like Hinson couldn't make sense of what Cage was doing, but there were exceptions. Pauline Kael, who was known for going against the grain of mainstream critical opinion, thought Cage was "airily amazing" in the film and observed that "he does some of the way-out stuff that you love actors in silent movies for doing."[6] Jonathan Rosenbaum, one of the most erudite film critics of his generation, also saw Cage's performance in a larger historical context: "What really makes this worth seeing is Cage's outrageously unbridled performance, which recalls such extravagant actorly exercises as Jean-Louis Barrault in Jean Renoir's *The Testament of Dr. Cordelier* and Jerry Lewis as Buddy Love in *The Nutty Professor*."[7] These critics understood that Cage's absolutely massive performance was not mere self-indulgent scenery chewing, but rather an attempt to do something bold with the art form.

Vampire's Kiss has not quite been assimilated into the canon as a previously unrecognized triumph in the way some of the other examples we discussed in earlier chapters have. Rather, it has developed a complex legacy. Cage cultists like me have long held it up as an unheralded masterpiece, but it hasn't (yet) managed to break through to a wider audience. Glancing at the most recent Rotten Tomatoes user reviews, Sarantos F. complains that it's "weird, unfunny and very messed up," while Darrell K. asks incredulously, "was this literally SUPPOSED to be a bad movie a la 'Sharknado,' or Ed Wood directed monstrosities or did Nicholas Cage [sic] actually feel like he was giving a great performance???" At the same time, however, *Vampire's Kiss* memes have flourished. A 9.5 minute supercut with the title, "Best Scenes from 'Vampire's Kiss'" has been viewed more than a million times on YouTube. Several still images and GIFs from the movie have become iconic. Although the film itself hasn't been embraced, the memes certainly have.

From the perspective of someone who takes *Vampire's Kiss* seriously as a work of art, this is a lamentable development. Taking all the biggest and loudest scenes out of context and viewing them as a supercut strips Cage's performance of its darkness and makes him look like a clown. I find it especially distasteful to take moments that are *not* funny when juxtaposed with the rape scene and recontextualize them so that they are good for a laugh. Cage does so much more in this movie than freak out. His performance is filled with subtle body language and other purposeful details. His smarmy, sniveling vision of yuppiedom is brilliant satire. The freakouts don't emerge from nowhere; they grow organically out of other elements of the performance. As Roger Ebert put it when discussing Cage's work in *Adaptation*: "No one else can project inner trembling so effectively."[8] But, alas, for the most part, *Vampire's Kiss* is seen not as the laboratory in which an ambitious young actor stretched the limits of his craft, but rather as a geek show where a wild and crazy guy put on an improvised spectacle. In interviews and commentaries over the years, Cage has repeatedly insisted that the performance is not composed of random outbursts but is in fact entirely deliberate: "It actually is extremely choreographed. Every one of those moves was thought out in my hotel room with my cat."[9] It's hard to imagine how anyone could doubt that Cage knew exactly what he was doing in *Vampire's Kiss*. One doesn't just slip on a banana peel and stumble into a performance like that.

So many of Cage's early performances deserve to be discussed, but in the interest of brevity the last one that I'll bring up is his turn as Sailor Ripley in David Lynch's Palme d'Or-winning *Wild at Heart*. If you've seen the movie, you know that the two most distinctive things about Sailor Ripley are that he wears a snakeskin jacket and he talks like Elvis. Remarkably, both of these things were Cage's ideas, not Lynch's. In a recent interview with none other than Marilyn Manson, Cage recounts the story:

> I was walking down Melrose Avenue and I went into a secondhand clothing store called Aardvark's Odd Ark, and bought this snakeskin jacket, because I wanted to be like Marlon Brando in Sidney Lumet's *The Fugitive Kind*. Then, in rehearsals, I had this epiphany. I was thinking about Andy Warhol, because I believe that what you can do in one art form, you can do in another. He took icons like Mick Jagger and Elvis Presley, and made collages out of them. I thought, 'Why can't you do that with a film performance?' And then I read the book *An Actor Prepares* by [Constantin] Stanislavski, and he said that the worst thing an actor can do is copy another actor. I thought it was a rule that should be broken in the spirit of creating a Warhol-like experience. I feel very lucky because David let me do it. And then I said, 'I'm going to talk like Elvis Presley. I think Sailor has some sort of a connection with Elvis, and that may be the

> source power that moves him.' And then he said, 'Okay, but you're going to have to sing a couple of Elvis songs.' I'm not a singer, but I said I'd do it. It was my way of giving him Cage, Warhol, Presley, and Brando in one performance.[10]

This is an illuminating glimpse into Cage's understanding of his own artistry. There's a synthetic element to his craft that involves bringing together unlikely influences in a way that both references their original cultural significance and transforms them into something new. In interviews and commentaries over the years, Cage has mentioned *many* influences beyond the ones we've already discussed. He's frequently brought up Kabuki, for instance, which is a traditional Japanese form of theater where actors rely on exaggerated, stylized movements to convey meaning to the audience. In *Raising Arizona*, he mimics Woody Woodpecker and Wile E. Coyote. In *Kick-Ass*, he borrows from Adam West's Batman. In *Ghost Rider: Spirit of Vengeance*, he emulates his pet cobras.

Cage's more referential performances invite us to reflect on the concepts of *celebrity* and *persona*—concepts that are also centrally significant in Warhol's work. In referencing Brando and Elvis in *Wild at Heart*, Cage didn't see himself as *copying* them, but rather as recontextualizing their personas to create new meaning. Sidney Lumet's *The Fugitive Kind*, co-written by Tennessee Williams, features Marlon Brando as a drifter who goes by the nickname "Snakeskin" on account of his jacket. Like Sailor Ripley, Brando's Snakeskin is ordered to leave town and stay away from the woman he loves under threat of violence, and also like Sailor, he refuses. By infusing Brando's persona into the role of Sailor, Cage emphasizes Tennessee Williams' influence on Lynch's screenplay and also finds continuity between Brando and Elvis.

Although Cage became a marquee name very early in his career, he didn't reach the apex of his stardom until after he won the Best Actor Oscar for his performance in Mike Figgis' indie drama, *Leaving Las Vegas*. The mainstream success of *Leaving Las Vegas* is surprising in retrospect. It is not exactly a crowd-pleaser, but it made 32 million dollars at the box office while costing only 4 million to produce. Cage plays an alcoholic screenwriter who has lost everything. He scrapes together all the money he can and heads to Las Vegas with the plan of drinking himself to death. Once this plan is underway he forms an unlikely and intense bond with a prostitute named Sera, played by Elisabeth Shue. Shue was best known at the time for appearing in family movies such as *The Karate Kid*, *Back to the Future*, and *Adventures in Babysitting*. As a kid who had grown up on these movies, it was shocking to hear her nonchalantly deliver lines in *Leaving Las Vegas* like: "You can fuck me in the ass. You can cum on my face. Just keep it out of my hair, I just washed it." Her character is often understood in terms of the archetype of the sex worker with a heart of gold, but that's a distorting oversimplification. Although she does treat Cage's character with unusual kindness, it's implied in a series of therapy sessions that her openness to being vulnerable with him is bound up with the terminal nature of their relationship. An explicit premise of their connection is that neither will try to steer the other off their self-destructive path; there is no real possibility of a long-term relationship between them. She is not his golden-hearted savior, but rather his double. While he ends up dead, she ends up homeless, having escaped her abusive pimp only to face the threat of violence every time she meets a client.

It's a bleak movie. It offers no redemption aside from the romantic gesture of two self-destructive people comforting one another on the way down. Cage's performance is in the same vein as *Vampire's Kiss*, but now it's framed by a grim alcoholic death spiral rather than the energetic absurdism of the earlier movie. This shift in framing made all the difference, as the same critics who panned his vampire shenanigans now praised his intensity. It is indeed a brilliant performance. He hired Tony Dingman, an actor who had fallen on hard times due to his alcoholism, as his "drinking coach." He studied the syncopated rhythms of Dingman's speech and his wobbling posture and strove for a level of authenticity that we rarely see in screen depictions of alcoholism. He even filmed a number of scenes stinking drunk, including the unscripted sequence where he has an outburst on the casino floor and flips over a blackjack table.

As Janet Maslin observes, writing for the *New York Times*: "Mr. Cage digs deep to find his character's inner demons while also capturing the riotous energy of his outward charm. The film would seem vastly more sordid without his irrepressible good humor."[11] While the film does have its share of Cage freakouts, it also lets him show off his range, extending from effervescent charisma to the deepest pits of despair. The seriousness of the film's themes prompted critics to view Cage's histrionics through a more charitable lens. He does a lot of the same things here that he does in *Vampire's Kiss*, but now they're seen as naked and fearless rather than laughable and ridiculous.

After Cage's Oscar win, he became one of the highest paid actors in Hollywood, appearing in action blockbusters including *The Rock* and *Con Air* as well as big budget romantic dramas *Captain Corelli's Mandolin* and *City of Angels*. Some of these performances are mild by Cage's standards, but they still reflect his idiosyncratic sensibility. He was interested at this stage of his career in expanding his range and trying different approaches to acting. Whereas his performance as Cameron Poe in *Con Air* is swaggering and heroic, he plays chemical weapons expert Stanley Godspeed in *The Rock* as a more reluctant figure who would rather be pushing paper in his office than trying to break into Alcatraz and foil a domestic terror plot. He brings surprising eccentricity to his role as the romantic lead in *Captain Corelli's Mandolin*, affecting the most ridiculous Italian accent anyone has ever done (roughly at the level of "it's-a-meeeeee ... Mario! I make-a-you a nice-a pizza pie!"). He takes *City of Angels* in the polar opposite direction. The film is a Hollywood remake of Wim Wenders' *Wings of Desire*—a German art film about an angel who chooses to forsake immortality and live a human life. Cage plays the central angel character (played by Bruno Ganz in the original) and pushes the role to the far extreme of quiet interiority. Say what one will about the movie (it's not my favorite), it's impressive to see an actor reach so far from the style they are associated with.

Cage incorporated discoveries from his *Vampire's Kiss* laboratory into a number of high-profile roles during the movie star stage of his career. After seeing John Woo's heroic bloodshed classic *Bullet in the Head*, he knew the Hong Kong maestro would let him go as far as he wanted, and so he really and truly went for it as terrorist Castor Troy in Woo's blockbuster *Face/Off*. For the first part of the movie, he's in grandiose *Vampire's Kiss* mode. But then the film's high concept premise kicks in and Cage's character switches faces with FBI agent Sean Archer, played by John Travolta. Cage thus plays a double role: first Castor Troy and then Sean Archer stuck in Troy's body. Since Archer must try to pass as Troy in order to foil his plans, Cage essentially plays John Travolta stuck in Nicolas Cage's body trying to impersonate Nicolas Cage. He's brilliant, and so is Travolta playing Cage stuck in Travolta's body trying to impersonate Travolta.

During this phase of his career, Cage also worked on a number of other prestigious projects, including *Adaptation*, written by Charlie Kaufman and directed by Spike Jonze, and *Bringing Out the Dead*, written by Paul Schrader and directed by Martin Scorsese. In *Adaptation*, he plays both neurotic, anxious Charlie Kaufman and his self-assured brother, Donald. He has repeatedly said that this was the greatest acting challenge of his career, not just because of the dual role, but also because the character of Charlie is so acutely against type for him. Donald was an easy fit, but playing a high strung, self-loathing introvert with writer's block required quite a transformation. He had to play roles at both ends of his range within the same movie. He aced it, and was nominated again for the Academy Award for Best Actor.

Bringing Out the Dead is another superb showcase of Cage's talent. He plays a burned out paramedic who hasn't saved anyone's life in months and has started seeing the ghosts of dead patients. He doesn't appear to have slept in a very long time and he carries the weight of infinite exhaustion on his face. Scorsese explained the qualities that led him to cast Cage in *Bringing Out the Dead* in an interview with Roger Ebert: "He's inventive and he goes from an expressive style, almost like silent film, like Lon Chaney, whom he adores, to something extremely internal."[12] Unsurprisingly, Scorsese gets it: Cage's expressionistic flair is only one side of what he does. His quiet side—and the way he moves between the two—is equally important. The memefication of Cage has distorted the popular understanding of this point.

As Cage's celebrity grew, his real-life antics became more and more eccentric. In a 2019 *New York Times* interview he explained: "I was very specific in my concept of who I wanted to be. I saw myself as a surrealist. This is going to sound pretentious, but I was, quote, trying to invent my own mythology, unquote, around myself."[13] He saw his *whole life* as a project in surrealism. As he became more and more successful, he spent his money in increasingly outrageous ways. He bought two king cobras, a shark, an octopus, a crocodile, and a dinosaur skull. While flirting with the idea of embarking on a quest to find the Holy Grail (literally), he travelled to Glastonbury to drink from a spring that's alleged to taste like blood and then followed a trail of historical references to Rhode Island. He found that he liked Rhode Island, so he bought expensive property there (and in many other places around the world, including a castle in Germany). He bought the Shah of Iran's Lamborghini and a giant pyramid-shaped tomb for himself in New Orleans. Amid these antics, he would periodically go on David Letterman or some other talk show and play up his eccentric persona, telling outlandish stories in his dynamic style. Recently, he's been in the news for a wonderful anecdote he related in his interview with Marilyn Manson:

> "The last time I gambled was about 30 years ago," Cage recalled. "I was in the Bahamas, and I walked into a casino and felt like I had my mojo with me, like nothing could go wrong. My game was roulette. I went in with $200, and I didn't miss a number, so much so that even the lady spinning the wheel said, 'Nothing sweeter than a repeater.' In 20 minutes I turned $200 into $20,000, so I went and found an orphanage in the Bahamas, met all the kids and the headmistress, and said, 'This is for you.' I put the 20 grand in her hand, walked away, and never gambled again, because if I did, it would ruin the power of that moment."[14]

This is not a man who leaves his work in the office: for Nicolas Cage, art is life and life is art. But, alas, Cage's real-life antics are a double-edged sword. On the one hand, he has created a mythology around himself that imbues his wilder performances with a sense of authenticity, but, on the other hand, the glut of wacky anecdotes have synergized with his memefication and bolstered his aura of clownishness. There is now a whole internet genre of Nicolas Cage clickbait: stuff like "9 Bizarre Facts about Nicolas Cage," or "Nicolas Cage's Craziest Fan Encounter Involved a Home Invasion and a Fudgesicle." Widespread reporting on the financial problems that Cage's extravagant spending created for him have led critics and the public to view nearly every career decision he makes in terms of his financial distress. Any time people don't immediately see the value of a project, they assume he took the job solely for a paycheck.

Cage's financial problems did indeed become critical in the mid-late 2000s. He owed the IRS millions of dollars and had overinvested in real estate in the years leading up to the Great Recession. At the same time, more and more of his films were met with an overwhelmingly negative critical response, including Neil Labute's remake of British folk horror classic *The Wicker Man* (which I will discuss at length below) and the Marvel Comics adaptation *Ghost Rider*. The latter—which features Cage drinking jelly beans out of a martini glass (while listening to The Carpenters and watching a video of a chimp doing karate) before becoming the flaming-skulled rider of Satan—made a tidy profit at the box office but critics smothered it with condescending takes: "For years scientists have theorized that one day Nicolas Cage would overact so badly that his head would burst into flames. Now, with *Ghost Rider*, the phenomenon has finally come to pass."[15]

In the following years, he started appearing in more and more movies with smaller and smaller budgets, many of which were direct-to-video. In 2018, he was in eight movies (including a documentary), and then another seven in 2019. This ongoing deluge of Cage has been a great source of delight for me, but not everyone sees it that way. Critic Morgan P. Salvo complains in his *Drive Angry* review: "Sure he's had some money problems, but when you're one of the biggest box office stars, why make crap after crap after crap? Now, strictly appearing in 'paycheck movies' there seems to always be a Nicolas Cage film happening somewhere."[16] Incredibly, this turns out to be a positive review: "Cage cannot single handedly destroy a movie this good, try as he might."

Most of Cage's output from his DTV period has been treated with similar derision, and critics have taken obvious delight in bringing up his earlier successes and gawking at how far he's fallen. Even wonky data analysis site fivethirtyeight.com got in on the fun and assembled a graph that plots Nicolas Cage movies according to box office take and Rotten Tomatoes score.[17] They divide his output into five categories, labeling his DTV work as "The Recession" and his poorly performing theatrical releases as "Not the bees!," which is a reference to an oft-mocked scene in the *Wicker Man* remake that I will discuss below. The small amount of positive attention these movies have gotten generally focuses on their meme-worthiness. Take, for instance, the 2017 crime movie *Arsenal*, in which Cage reprises his utterly bonkers role from his brother Christopher Coppola's 1993 crime film *Deadfall*. Every serious Cage fan has long lamented the brevity of his *Deadfall* performance, and *Arsenal* feels like a gift from the gods. Many critics could only see the memes. One negative Tomato review reads: "The kind of film that serves only to add to YouTube supercuts of

Cage freaking out."[18] Another echoes the same thought: "Is there a better way to ring in a new year of movies with some more material to add to the Nicolas Cage 'Losing His S*** Montage'?"[19]

Cage explained his selection criteria for DTV roles in his 2019 *New York Times* interview: "I can't go into specifics or percentages or ratios, but yeah, money is a factor. I'm going to be completely direct about that. There's no reason not to be. There are times when it's more of a factor than not. I still have to feel that, whether or not the movie around me entirely works, I'll be able to deliver something and be fun to watch." While Cage's financial trouble has led him to be less picky, he's still tried to stick to roles that give him the opportunity to do something worthwhile. One thing that few commentators seem to recognize is that Cage has a long history of taking projects below his pay grade for creative reasons. Just before winning the Oscar, at a point in his career where he was making millions of dollars for starring roles, he appeared as the villain in Barbet Schroeder's neo-noir *Kiss of Death*, getting third billing after Samuel L. Jackson and David frickin' Caruso. Having just appeared as the leading man in several romantic comedies, he explained: "I needed to get back to the other kind of work that I like to do." He plays seething, buffed-up gangster Little Junior Brown, a performance that Roger Ebert described as "the weirdest villain since Dennis Hopper slithered into *Blue Velvet*." The first time we meet him, he's bench-pressing an exotic dancer. It's superb Cage, and it suggests a more favorable way to view his DTV output: these movies have given him the opportunity to "get back to the other kind of work he likes to do," namely, the experimentation of his early days.

As I argued in Chapter 3, low-budget DTV movies have the advantage of affording a high degree of creative freedom.

DTV releases don't need to appeal to a mass audience; they are for the sort of bottom feeder (like myself) who will pay six bucks to see literally anything with Nicolas Cage in it. And that's a good thing! Cage's DTV output has been an absolute feast of exploratory acting. Low-profile releases *Army of One* and *Between Worlds* feature two of his most hilariously outlandish performances. He's also experimented in subtler ways. In his 2019 *New York Times* interview, he explains that when he stretched out the phrase "You talked!" into a bizarrely protracted yell in 2014's *Rage*, he intended to create a "Stockhausen effect," which is a reference to the innovations in dissonance of avant-garde composer Karlheinz Stockhausen. Granted, *Rage* is not in the top tier of his DTV output, but Tomato critics have been entirely oblivious to what he tries to do with the performance. Isaac Feldberg writes: "Nicolas Cage takes 'paycheck movie' to a whole new level in *Rage*, a completely worthless, contemptible excuse for a revenge actioner."[20] Gary Goldstein has a similar take: "The latest in a parade of cheesy, derivative action-thrillers that erstwhile A-list actor Nicolas Cage has recently starred in, presumably as a quick cash grab."[21] And then Pat Padua gives us another example of the tendency to evaluate Cage movies in terms of meme potential: "Would not have been saved by more of those over-the-top Cage moments, but it would have helped."[22]

But doesn't the story I've been telling suggest a different way to understand *Rage*? The movie is a riff on the *Taken* formula, where a father with a talent for violence pursues the criminals who kidnapped his daughter. Cage's performance is not a wall-to-wall explosion of the sort that would generate lots of clips for YouTube supercuts. Rather, he leans into his character's grief and his cold capacity for violence. The performance is understated in a way you wouldn't expect if you think of

Cage primarily in terms of freakouts. It's not *all* understated: he certainly *does* freak out (in a way that references Karlheinz Stockhausen), and these high voltage moments have more impact because of their contrast with his overall portrayal of the character. But this was never going to be a movie that Tomato critics like. It's not for them. It's a mean, exploitative riff on a well-worn formula, and although it takes this formula in an unusual direction, it doesn't even attempt to jump through the hoops that it would need to jump through to get a Fresh rating on the Tomatometer. That doesn't mean it can't be good.

Perhaps none of Cage's DTV efforts more clearly reveals how poorly most critics understand him than 2018's *Looking Glass*, directed by veteran Tim Hunter. I find *Rage* pleasantly sleazy, but the sleaze in *Looking Glass* is top shelf. It opens with ominous driving and credits in a David Lynch font. We learn that married couple Nicolas Cage and Robin Tunney are struggling with grief after losing their only daughter and have purchased a scuzzy motel off Craigslist in the hope of starting a new life. The hook is that Cage finds a secret passageway to a two-way mirror through which he can spy on guests. His performance is relatively understated, without a lot of screaming and yelling, but if you know what to look for in a quieter Cage performance, it's wondrous. For most of the movie, whenever he's not looking through the spy mirror, he's *thinking* about looking through the spy mirror. The distracting obsession is all over his face. When he *is* looking through the spy mirror, he brilliantly conveys the thrill as well as the shame of voyeurism without saying a word. The movie is a veritable gallery of fantastic reaction shots; my favorite is his alarmed expression after waking up from an especially messed up dream. The progression of these shots builds tension as his secret erotic obsession grows, and this tension is abruptly released in the film's disarmingly raw sex scenes.

Looking Glass is one of my favorite titles from the last decade of Cage's career, and other Cage fans I'm acquainted with feel similarly, but critics don't even seem to begin to grasp the way the movie might look to someone who takes it seriously. Eric Kohn of *Indiewire*, for instance, really does not get it: "The result is a hollow vehicle that Cage simply floats through on autopilot, and as he peers through a mirror at a more exciting world beyond his grasp, it's impossible not to relate."[23] Frank Swietek wants more memes: "A sadly muted thrill-free thriller, starring a disappointingly manic-deprived Cage."[24] Todd Jorgenson agrees: "The ubiquitous Cage is more understated than usual these days, which is a drawback since that consequently spotlights the uninspired film's tedious incoherence."[25] These takes illustrate the damage that Cage's memefication has wrought: his experimentation continues to evolve, but critics are looking for him to rehash his greatest hits. Unless one of his movies either has the superficial trappings of artistic credibility or something to add to the YouTube highlight reel, it's dismissed out of hand without serious consideration of what he's trying to do.

Amid his DTV period, Cage did have two notable critical successes: Werner Herzog's *Bad Lieutenant: Port of Call New Orleans* and David Gordon Green's *Joe*. He's said that these were two of his favorite roles, and indeed his performances in both are magnificent. *Bad Lieutenant* gave him the opportunity to pay homage to one of his most significant influences: erstwhile Herzog regular Klaus Kinski, an actor who is legendary for his surreal style and violent intensity. *Joe*, in contrast, features one of Cage's most naturalistic performances. He plays a loner ex-con and foreman of a work crew who hires and reluctantly befriends a young boy with an alcoholic father. It's reminiscent of Clint Eastwood movies such as *A Perfect World* or *Gran Torino*, and Cage plays it with Eastwood-esque brooding virility. Critics ate it up, but, unfortunately, they praised it at the expense of his other work. Eleanor Ringle writes: "After slumming for years in crud like 'Ghost Rider' and 'The Sorcerer's Apprentice,' Nicolas Cage has decided to remind himself—and all of us—that, yes, he can act, That, in fact, he's a helluva an actor when he puts his mind to it."[26]

There was some dissent to this narrative. Critic Nick Schager defended Cage's less popular work, but did so at the expense of *Joe*:

> Cage's performance is a soulful, forceful turn that, while benefiting from his larger-than-life aura, is far more muted than much of his recent output. And that makes it one of the actor's least interesting roles to date. Because Nic Cage's superstardom is predicated on his idiosyncratic craziness, his loony sense of humor, his hair-trigger volatility. He's in his element when he's allowed to be uninhibited. Frazzled and freaky. Screaming-mad and bug-eyed rowdy. Chewing scenery like a man who hasn't eaten in weeks.[27]

Both sides miss the point. *Joe* isn't as disconnected from Cage's other recent work as critics suppose. There has *never* been a point in his career when he was content to repeat himself. He's *always* experimented with different approaches to different roles, and *Joe* is a part of this pattern.

Look through his filmography and you'll see that any time he's turned in consecutive manic performances, he's then shifted gears and done something totally different for his next role. Cage has always moved between different acting styles—sometimes within a single film. Method acting, Western Kabuki, Nouveau Shamanism, Jerry Lewis, Elvis, cartoon characters, quiet introspection: he's done it all. *Joe* is a foray into naturalism, and it's a tour de force. Rather than merely eliciting a begrudging acknowledgement that he's capable of good acting, it should prompt his detractors to look harder at the works they've underestimated.

This brings us to the last stage in our history of Nicolas Cage: the comeback. Although Cage's DTV period has been the target of relentless critical derision, it was also the era when his memefication flourished. While this process has attracted a great deal of shallow, condescending attention from gawkers who want to see our man freak out, it has also created many new fans and led some to a deeper exploration of his work. The internet today abounds with Nicolas Cage fan culture. Reddit user u/schwano, for instance, posted a popular thread titled "Nicolas Cage made 29 direct-to-video movies in the 2010s. I watched all of them."[28] He includes capsule reviews of Cage's entire DTV output, and while I don't agree with all of his views, his reviews are attentive to the particular values that DTV movies are capable of achieving and they are sympathetic to what Cage is trying to do. The AV Club posted a condescending article about this enterprise: "Foolhardy Redditor reviews every direct-to-video Nic Cage movie from the past decade."[29] They make it into a big joke about the bravery it must have taken to trudge through all of this dreck, but, of course, they don't even imagine the possibility that a lot of us have been eagerly keeping up with these movies all along.

This combination of memefication and a growing cult of fandom set the stage for the warm reception of Panos Cosmatos' trippy horror-revenge film *Mandy*. *Mandy* found the perfect recipe to make Cage relevant to a hip indie audience: a young director with a lot of hype, title cards in a heavy metal font, a synth score from Jóhann Jóhannsson, neon lighting, fantasy references aplenty, and Cage flipping the fuck out. My feed (which the algorithm has correctly determined should include every single article having to do with Nicolas Cage) was full of clickbait headlines like "*Mandy* First Look: Cage goes Full Cage," and "The Trailer for Nicolas Cage's New Movie Must Be Seen to Be Believed."

The marketing and buzz surrounding *Mandy* marked a new phase in Cage's career: the viral celebration of his persona as a viable marketing strategy. Both through his acting work and his real-life shenanigans, Cage has built the image of a wildly unpredictable madman who will absolutely rampage through a movie when given the opportunity. Memefication inflated this image to the level of cultural icon. Not many people have seen *Vampire's Kiss*, but a whole lot of people have seen the memes and supercuts. *Mandy* has been sold in terms of this persona: it's a chance to see Cage go all the way.

He plays Red, a logger who lives in the woods with his girlfriend, Mandy. Their lifestyle is idyllic until it's interrupted by an LSD-addled hippie cult led by a Charles Manson figure named Jeremiah Sand. After she laughs at Sand's penis and a folk song he's written about himself, the cult burns Mandy alive, leading Red to go on a bloody rampage of vengeance. One of the movie's most remarkable scenes happens after Mandy is killed, when Red frees himself from the barbed wire that was used to restrain him and stumbles into his now empty house to face the unthinkable new reality that Mandy is dead. The moment when we first face the fact that someone we love is gone and never coming back is one of the most brutal things a human being ever experiences. It's no small thing to convey the emotional devastation of this moment in a way that is legible to the audience. Cage goes *all in*. He violently chugs a bottle of vodka and lets out a series of guttural bellows and primal screams. It's an earthshaking bit of acting.

Unfortunately, many audiences laughed. In his 2019 *New York Times* interview, he brings up this reaction in response to a question about the interplay of sincerity and irony in his work:

> I have gone out of my way not to be ironic and—with the risk of looking ridiculous—to be genuinely emotionally naked. And that gets uncomfortable. There were times where people saw 'Mandy,' and I was having to break down in a scene, and people were laughing. They don't know how to handle it. But that's not ironic, that's naked, which is embarrassing for people.[30]

The clear antecedent to this scene in Cage's body of work is the gut-wrenching scene in *Leaving Las Vegas* when he chugs vodka and dry heaves in the sink after waking up with acute delirium tremens. The corresponding scene in *Mandy* is not an obvious place to laugh. It's a visceral expression of grief, and such expressions are rarely funny. Audiences laugh because they are primed and hoping for him to freak out, and this is one mother of a freakout. Cage's diagnosis is that the audience's laughter reflects embarrassment at his emotional nakedness. While context is also relevant (no one laughed at the emotional nakedness in *Leaving Las Vegas*), his point is important. Private expressions of grief can be ridiculous. When no one is looking and we are in unbearable emotional pain, we are capable of all manner of abject bellowing. I've been there. We aren't used to seeing this sort of private moment on screen, and it's easier to laugh than to absorb such an uncomfortably sincere emotional display.

The revenge portion of *Mandy* sees Cage return to the sort of referential, synthetic acting that was characteristic of his early work. Initially, he fights with an agile style and makes a clear reference to Bruce Lee after breaking an opponent's neck. Later, he samples a bad batch of LSD and transforms into a hybrid of Jason Voorhees and the golem of Jewish legend (depicted in the 1920 German Expressionist film *The Golem: How He Came into the World*).

Cage's performance in *Mandy* has a high degree of continuity with the rest of his career. Like most of his expressionistic work, it's downstream of *Vampire's Kiss*. It's a higher profile production than his DTV projects, but certainly no more prestigious than *Joe* or *Bad Lieutenant: Port of Call New Orleans*. Critics and commentators, however, saw it as a radical break with his recent output. Critic Daniel Barnes, for example, quipped: "Nicolas Cage offers his once-a-decade reminder of why we ever cared."[31]

Why did *Mandy* elicit this sort of reaction? I suggest that it's because marketing and buzz around the film presented it as a consummation of Cage's meme legacy, which prompted critics and audiences to view the film through the lens of ironic detachment (to be clear, I don't believe this was Cosmatos' intention). Hardly anyone commenting on *Mandy* mentions the emotional weight of Cage's performance. Most everyone instead focuses on the fact that he goes plenty nuts. The narrative is, "if you love the memes, you'll love this movie." The same trend continued with Richard Stanley's 2019 Lovecraft adaptation *Color Out of Space*. In some respects, it has a similar recipe to *Mandy*: neon lighting, a synth-heavy score from a respected composer (Colin Stetson this time), and lots of Cage flipping out. This time he mostly rehashes bits and pieces of *Vampire's Kiss*, *Army of One*, and *Mom and Dad*. This film bolstered the narrative of Cage's neon-synth comeback. Cage is now seen as being "in on the joke" (it's hard to believe there was ever a doubt), and his upcoming projects are getting more and more buzz of the sort that surrounded *Mandy*: "This New Nicolas Cage Trailer Must Be Seen to be Believed!"

Cage has continued to work at a prolific pace, except now people are looking forward to his new releases. And there's plenty to look forward to: the man has a lot of movies coming out. I'm so in. But I've been in all along. I just hope that sooner or later his work is able to tear through the tawdry shroud of memes that so often obscures the true nature of his greatness.

***

With the history I've just presented, I've tried to undermine the dominant narrative that Cage's career has been a roller-coaster of artistic highs and lows. While I acknowledge that he's made some bad movies (and not the good kind ... ahem, *The Humanity Bureau*), his career has been characterized first and foremost by an enduring spirit of experimentation and a willingness to take creative risks. He started as a zealous young actor wanting to bring German Expressionism to 1980s Hollywood, went on to become one of the highest paid movie stars in the world, morphed into a critical punching bag who took on low-prestige projects and did something remarkable with them, and has finally begun to reclaim his rightful place as an icon of cinema.

I want to return now to the suggestion that there's something arbitrary about the way Cage performances are sorted by critics into the honorific category that includes *Leaving Las Vegas*, *Face/Off*, and *Mandy* and the derisive category that includes *Rage*, *The Wicker Man*, and *Looking Glass*. I've already begun to make this case by showing that there is far more continuity in Cage's career than critics typically acknowledge. I now return to my initial suggestion that the dismissive stance that critics have adopted towards large swathes of his output is grounded in a failure of imagination.

At the beginning of this chapter, I complained about critic Gary M. Kramer's myopic claim that Cage doesn't go as "bat-shit crazy" in *Grand Isle* as his fans would like. Let's turn now to the thoughts of an actual Nicolas Cage fan—someone who has explored his body of work in a thoughtful and open-minded way. I'm speaking of Lindsay Gibb, author of the 2015 monograph *National Treasure: Nicolas Cage*. The book is a heroic effort; it presents a well-researched and extensively detailed argument that Nicolas Cage is a great actor, and that his greatness extends to many of the roles that are often disrespected by critics.

Gibb begins with an explanation of how she got started on the project. It's an explanation that will be all too familiar to any serious Nicolas Cage fan. She became frustrated with constantly having to defend her love of Cage against the insistence that, aside from his few critically sanctioned roles, he's *obviously* a bad actor. She reports in despair (and I can relate) that friends often assume that she's being a contrarian and defending Cage in bad faith. This is how strong the grip of received norms and popular perceptions can be: they give rise to the presumption that anyone with an outlying point of view is faking it to troll their friends. But Gibb is *clearly* not faking it. I was delighted as I read the book to feel a sense of kinship with someone who totally gets what's up with Nicolas Cage. In Ted Cohen's terms, we are members of the same affective community.

She argues:

> Cage is experimental in the decidedly unexperimental terrain of Hollywood feature films. He looks to

> unconventional styles of acting (and even other forms of art) for inspiration. His disparate choices of roles are construed as a meandering, paycheck-inspired career, rather than experiments with genre or proof that despite his singularity, and his notoriety, he can embody almost anyone. When the easiest and potentially most successful career move would have been to remain in genres that have been lucrative and critically respected, Cage instead chooses films that will make him uncomfortable and challenge his approach to acting ... Never one to rest on his laurels or phone in performances, Cage consistently encourages viewers to question our assumptions and expectations about actors and acting, about art in general. And above all, he's always trying. And that what makes him great. He's earnest even when it would be cooler not to care.[32]

Preach. I have some more general thoughts about the significance of Gibb's book, but first I want to take a closer look at the movie that marked the beginning of the transition from his movie star phase to his DTV period: *The Wicker Man* (2006).

Robin Hardy's original 1973 version of *The Wicker Man* is one of the best-loved British horror movies. It tells the story of a police investigator who travels to a remote island in the Hebrides to investigate the disappearance of a young girl. He discovers that the island is controlled by a pagan clan who he suspects of practicing human sacrifice. It turns out that the young girl's disappearance was staged to lure him to the island and that *he* is the one who's to be sacrificed. It's the sort of classic that no one wants to see remade, but American playwright and filmmaker Neil Labute remade it anyways. Labute is best known for edgy black comedies that satirize gender relations, including *In the Company of Men* and *Your Friends and Neighbors*. His *Wicker Man* remake was a resounding critical failure, earning five Razzie nominations, including Worst Picture and Worst Actor. It's widely considered the point when Cage jumped the shark.

When the film was released, I thought (like everyone else) that *The Wicker Man* should not have been remade. I disliked Labute's film overall, but I did enjoy the absurd ending, where Cage dons a bear suit and abruptly punches a hippie woman in the face before being burnt alive. In the unrated cut that was released on DVD, a deleted scene was added that would go on to become synonymous with Cage's perceived downfall. It's emphasized throughout the movie that his character is deathly allergic to bees. In the deleted scene, part of a pagan ritual, his captors put a cage over his head and fill it with bees. He infamously bellows: "NO, NOT THE BEES! NOT THE BEES! AAAARRGH! MY EYES! MY EYES! AAAAAAAAARRGH!" It has become de rigueur in every negative review of a DTV Cage release to bring this moment up while bemoaning his career trajectory.

Incredibly, the majority of critics assume that the humor of *The Wicker Man* is unintentional. Here are two examples:

MaryAnn Johanson: "I'd look more kindly on Neil LaBute's profoundly silly movie—his first foray into anything like big-budget filmmaking geared toward a mainstream audience—if I thought he meant any of it in jest, if any of it were winking at us even a little."[33]

Scott Nash: "I won't give the ending away except to say that it is hilarious. This is unintentional of course, but funny, nonetheless. Just picture Nicolas Cage fighting off a bunch of flower-power women while wearing a bear costume and trying to earn the Razzie for the most overacting in a movie award at the same time."[34]

These takes are utterly baffling. Have you ever seen a Nicolas Cage movie before? You think the absurdist humor of the ending is *unintentional*???? Nicolas Cage puts a bear suit on and punches a woman in the face before having a "NOT THE BEES!" conniption and you don't think this is supposed to be funny? Frankly, if that's your take, I don't know if I can help you.

For those who are able to recognize the plain fact that *The Wicker Man* is intentionally comical, however, I have some thoughts. As a dyed-in-the-wool Cage fan, I periodically rewatch most of his movies, and over time *The Wicker Man* has grown on me. I now think that it's a very interesting remake and that Cage's performance is compelling throughout the movie. The key step that led to this change of heart was making an active effort to understand what the movie is trying to do instead of simply comparing it to the original *Wicker Man* and finding it lacking. I only got to this step because I was willing to first embrace it in its perceived badness and continue to engage with it.

In the original British version, the background conflict is between Christianity and paganism. The protagonist is devoutly Christian and his posture towards the pagan islanders reeks of cultural arrogance. He expects to be celebrated as the missing child's savior, and the revelation of the true reason he's been lured to the island is a symbolic comeuppance for Christian arrogance. In Labute's version, the religious conflict is deemphasized and Cage's character is not portrayed as devout. This should lead us to ask: what replaces Christianity as the movie's thematic target? I propose that it's the same as Labute's other movies from this period: gender.

In Labute's version, the pagan clan is a matriarchy. Some critics have suggested that the movie is about the dangers of female power. That seems … unlikely. The movie's thematic orientation is clear: whereas in the original the arrogance driving the protagonist was bound up with Christianity, here it's Cage's sociocultural power trifecta of being a white male cop. He is easily lured from California to the Puget Sound by a damsel in distress who needs help finding another damsel in distress. As he tries to find a seaplane pilot willing to give him a lift to the island, he is repeatedly told that outsiders are not welcome there. He doesn't care at all, however, and when he arrives, he doesn't even attempt a subtle entrance. He tromps in waving his badge, barking orders, and making demands. Being from California, he has no jurisdiction, but he just bullishly acts as though he does. This aspect of Cage's performance has baffled audiences. He is initially situated as the hero of the movie, but as his investigation progresses he is presented as increasingly incompetent and unlikable. He stated in a 2013 interview with the *Guardian* that he wanted to grow a handlebar mustache and wear an extra-stiff suit, which would have made it easier for audiences to see what he was going for: a comically arrogant cop who embodies male entitlement.

The matriarchal colony exploits his arrogance to manipulate him every step of the way. The ending—where Cage is burned alive as a ritual sacrifice—is triumphant and cathartic. The film is a black comedy and a satire of gender relations (which is what anyone who had been following Labute's career *should* have expected), and the ending goes in a comically absurd direction for a reason: the white male cop—the avatar of dominant authority—is made ridiculous. Cage wanted to push it even further. In Roger Corman's 1964 film *The Masque of Red Death*, satanic aristocrats are dealt a gruesome comeuppance through the combined efforts of oppressed servants and the grim reaper. The resident jester tricks a particularly cruel nobleman played by Patrick Magee into putting on an ape suit, ties him up, humiliates him in front of his noble peers, and then lights him on fire. The image of this vicious asshole burning to death in an ape suit is thematically central to the movie, which—like both versions of *The Wicker Man*—is about the blind arrogance of power. Cage wanted to reference this moment by keeping the bear suit on as he's burned alive. This clearly would have been an improvement, if only Labute had matched him in artistic courage.

Critic James Berardinelli complains: "In the 1973 movie, Edward Woodward's performance as the visiting policeman was peerless. Nicolas Cage is a woeful replacement. His delivery is stiff and the character comes across as absurd. Given the right role, Cage can be effective, but this is a case of miscasting."[35] This is a clear example of a failure of critical imagination. Berardinelli is right that Cage's performance is stiff and that his character comes across as absurd. But he doesn't consider *why* Cage and Labute would have taken the character in this direction. He assumes it's a *mistake*, as if Labute were going for something else and inadvertently ended up with a stiff and absurd performance at the center of his movie because he made the error of casting Nic Cage. Berardinelli has a narrow idea of what a police investigator performance should be like—a preconception derived from received norms for investigative procedurals—and he brusquely dismisses Cage's performance because it sharply clashes with this expectation.

One of the negative takes quoted above wishes that the movie would have "winked" at the audience to let us know that it's supposed to be funny (recall that Hal Hinson had a similar complaint about *Vampire's Kiss*). The implication is that there are ways of letting the audience know that you're joking, and that *The Wicker Man's* absurdity would be more palatable if it had done so. I could not disagree more strongly. For one thing, you don't need to wink when you've got Nicolas Cage in a bear suit punching a woman in the face. But, further, to the extent that the movie is ambiguous, that makes it more interesting. As I argued in Chapter 1, obscure authorial intention can be especially compelling. *The Wicker Man* plays with our expectations. It is standard in the genre for the audience to identify with the investigator protagonist, and the movie uses this expectation to its advantage by getting us to identify with Cage's entitled perspective before reversing the power dynamic and leaving us to reflect on *why* we identified with the arrogant white male cop by default. The film doesn't tip its hand too early—its absurdity builds incrementally before exploding in the climax. A wink would have ruined it.

Is *The Wicker Man* a good-bad movie? Is Cage's performance a good-bad performance? In his 2019 *New York Times* interview, Cage was asked to define good and bad acting. His response is perfect:

> It can be a very blurry line. I've seen some horrible acting that I think is wonderful ... it cracks me up, and I don't want to mention names, but in film acting you can do things that seem erratic or out of touch or not in sync, but it's a valid stylization as long as you anchor it within the context of the character and situation. When you listen to Stockhausen's "Punkte," or "Stimmung" or "Mantra"—it's all these voices and quick, snappy chords that seem discordant to a point and as if they don't make any sense. Yet it is of a piece and does belong together. Similarly, you can read a script and go: "Why would a character do that? That doesn't make any sense." But people are like weather vanes. We don't always blow in the same direction. Sometimes you do things that there's no explanation

> for other than that we're human, and that can apply within a performance. So can I get back to your question? What is good acting? What is bad acting? [Lawrence] Olivier had his argument, but look at James Cagney in "White Heat." "Made it, Ma! Top of the world!" That's not "real." But is it fun to watch? Is it exciting? Is it truthful? Yeah, and to me, that is great acting. It's a matter of which paintbrush you want to work with. I can look at TV commercials and see cringeworthy acting, and it makes me laugh, and I'm probably going to wind up putting it in one of my performances. I mean, I've done it.[36]

This answer is very much in line with the picture I've been developing in this book: the line between good and bad acting is much blurrier than the critical consensus supposes. "Horrible" acting—even acting that makes us cringe—can be wonderful. When he mentions TV commercials, he's referring in particular to a John Stamos pantyhose ad that he emulated in *Peggy Sue Got Married*. Acting decisions like this are hard to makes sense of within the framework of received norms, but they nonetheless have the potential for brilliance.

It is understandable that *The Wicker Man* has been received as a bad movie. It transgresses received norms in a way that lacks an aura of artistic seriousness. But it's possible to possess such an aura without in fact being artistically serious and it's possible to be artistically serious and yet be denied the aura. Are Jeff Koons' balloon animal sculptures artistically serious? I have my doubts, but they sell for 91 million dollars. Conversely, there's more to Labute's film than meets the eye. I don't think it's a *great* film, but it certainly doesn't deserve its abysmal reputation. Consider by way of contrast Bruno Dumont's absurdist investigative procedurals *Li'l Quinquin*,

Slack Bay, and *Coincoin and the Extra-Humans*. These films, unlike *The Wicker Man*, were immediately classified as avant-garde. This was an obvious categorization for two reasons: first, Dumont had already built an aura of artistic seriousness around himself through successful showings at high profile film festivals and so on, and second, these films push their absurdity so far that there can be no possible question about what they're going for. *The Wicker Man* isn't exactly subtle, but it builds its absurdity more gradually than Dumont's films do. More importantly, Labute was already considered a marginal director by many and Cage had an (unfair) reputation for undisciplined acting. Because of these preconceptions, the default was to consider it a bad movie. But there is time yet for its reputation to be rehabilitated.

Cage was asked in his 2019 *New York Times* interview how he thinks his life's work will be remembered. He responded: "I think time is a friend. Many of my movies that were mocked are enjoying a renaissance. So I'm hopeful that time will be on my side."[37] But how does a renaissance like that happen?

This is where Bad Movie Lovers have a role to play. Bad Movie Love is about finding values that fall outside the horizon of the critical imagination. There's the pseudo-modernism of *Plan 9 from Outer Space*, the formalist beauty of a sweaty Scotty Adkins fight scene, the quirkiness of Dolph Lundgren's acting, the lively humor of *Twilight*, and—I propose—the absurdist genre deconstruction of *The Wicker Man*. When it was initially released, I was right there with the critics. I really had no need for another Neil Labute movie in my life, neither did I care to see another remake of a 1970s horror classic. I was certainly a Nicolas Cage fan, but my understanding of what he's all about was still at an early stage of development. I was only able to progress to the point where I could see what's compelling about

The Wicker Man because I was open to continuing to engage with it on the basis of my (limited) interest in Cage's performance. At first, I thought his acting was good-bad. I didn't see that there was much of a point to the way he played the role, but it amused me for this very reason. This amusement sustained my engagement, eventually leading me to a richer understanding of what the movie is about and why Cage played the role the way he did. This progression mirrors my relationship with the *Twilight* series: initially I thought it was bad, then I thought it was good *because* it was bad, and then finally I realized that at least some aspects of it are just plain good. Embracing the movie as good-bad was a necessary intermediate stage that cleared away the prejudices that shaped my initial impressions. This is one way that the rehabilitation of a poorly received movie can begin. Bad Movie Lovers—who we must remember are also highly likely to favor the avant-garde—excavate values that are not initially obvious. This has been happening for *Freddy Got Fingered* and it might yet happen for *The Wicker Man*. In 2016, *Vampire's Kiss* screened at the Museum of Modern Art, which is good sign that we are well on our way.

Bad Movie Lovers constitute a kind of critical vanguard. We rifle through bargain DVD bins and the dark corners of disreputable streaming services looking for neglected gems. We actively seek out the movies that get the *worst* reviews, because we know that a Rotten Tomatoes score below 10% doesn't mean what it's supposed to mean. We find values that others miss. The joys and satisfactions of this hunt will be a theme of my concluding chapter, but for now I want to highlight the way that film culture as a whole benefits from it. We do our part to drive the ongoing expansion and rehabilitation of the received canon. The world has a clique of film students in LA to thank for saving *The Room* from obscurity. Fan criticism like

Gibb's book and untold numbers of podcasts and blogs has made an important contribution to the rehabilitation of Nicolas Cage's legacy. There are many other people like Gibb out there championing film artists with poor critical reputations. Will Sloan and Justin Decloux, for instance, produce a podcast called *The Important Cinema Club* and have published *tons* of material (including whole books) examining the work of maligned or neglected film artists such as Albert Pyun and Joe D'Amato. They juxtapose this material with discussion of revered canonical filmmakers like Hou Hsiao-Hsien in a way that highlights the overlap between Bad Movie Love and highbrow cinephilia. The term "vulgar auteurism" is sometimes used to refer to the critical stance that takes seriously the artistry of filmmakers working outside the perceived boundaries of art cinema. I prefer to think of it as plain old auteurism, as I suspect that "vulgar" marks a distinction without a difference, but in any case it's an important movement. Film scholar Peter Labuza relates the vulgar auteurist movement to the category of "Eccentric Esoterica" introduced by Andrew Sarris, the primary critic who brought French auteurist theory to America.[38] There is a whole universe out there of highbrow auteurist writings on widely disrespected directors such as Michael Bay, Paul W. S. Anderson, and M. Night Shyamalan. The cinephiles behind these writings are doing the Lord's work.

There's an episode in Season 5 of the TV series *Community* in which the character of Abed (a movie buff) takes a class on Nicolas Cage and has a breakdown over his inability to figure out whether Cage is a good actor or a bad actor. His worldview strictly entails that every actor must be either good or bad, but Cage doesn't compute: "He's a complex performer. He'll give you *The Rock*, *Con Air*, then *Face/Off*, and you think you understand, but then *Windtalkers*, *Guarding Tess*, *The Wicker Man*.

He begs you to stop watching, but you can't." The joke plays on the ambivalence many feel towards Cage. Pretty much everyone agrees that he's great in some movies, which makes it hard for people to understand his stranger choices. But the Nicolas Cage whom everyone loves and the Nicolas Cage whom so many people mock are the same Nicolas Cage—intrepid experimentalist and trampler of received norms. It's so hard to determine if he's good or bad because he's both and neither: he's good-bad and he's great. But his badness is bound up with fleeting convention. It's his greatness that will echo in the ages.

Value of art

- in its own right
- For a person

Bad Movies and the Good Life

Six

Friends, we arrive at my closing statement.

There's a lot of great art out there, too much to consume in a single lifetime. Why should we spend our precious time watching bad movies? In this chapter, I'll make the case that bad movies have a place in the good life. This will require getting into broader questions about the value of art. We will begin by revisiting the question of what it means for art to be good or bad in light of the picture that has developed over the course of this book.

***

In Chapter 1, I suggested two different ways that the terms "good" and "bad" are used in reference to art:

Final sense: artworks are good or bad according to whether or not they are worthwhile.
Conventional sense: artworks are good or bad according to conventional standards and norms.

There's a further distinction we need to think about. On the one hand, there's the value that an artwork has *in its own right*, and, on the other hand, there's the value that an artwork has

DOI: 10.4324/9780367808969-6

for a person. But why think that art has value in its own right? Why not think that the value of art is just the value it has for particular people?

We don't *randomly* value art, we value certain artworks for certain reasons, and these reasons track the features the artworks have in their own right. A clear sign of this is that when we engage with art, we make an effort to get it right. We strive to correct or confirm judgments we are unsure about and contest other peoples' judgments when we think they are mistaken.

Consider Christopher Nolan's film *Memento*. The gimmick of *Memento* is that the narrative is presented in reverse order. It starts with the end of the story and works back to the beginning. Suppose you watch the movie with a friend and after it ends your friend says: "That movie made no sense. Characters die in one scene but then they are alive in later scenes." You realize that somehow your friend didn't understand that the narrative is in reverse order. It's no surprise that they didn't like the movie if this is how they interpreted it. Isn't it perfectly appropriate to argue with their evaluation? "I don't think that's fair; the movie is in reverse order, and so the reason characters die in one scene and then are alive in a later scene is that the later scene actually happens earlier in the narrative chronology." Suppose your friend replies: "I disagree! The movie is not in reverse order, it's just bad." Their judgment is incorrect: the movie might be bad, but it's surely not bad for this reason. If it's possible for evaluations of art to be incorrect, then the value of an artwork isn't simply a matter of how much we happen to value it.

One might think (and many surely do) that the value an artwork has in its own right depends on whether it's good bad in the conventional sense, and that when Bad Movie

Lovers find bad movies worthwhile, they're not really valuing them in their own right, but rather inventing some other way of engaging with them that they find worthwhile.

This can't be right, however. Bad Movie Lovers love *some* bad movies, and they love them because of their distinct qualities. I love *Batman & Robin*, but I do not particularly enjoy the 2005 version of *The Fantastic Four*. Both of these are conventionally bad superhero movies, but I love the one and not the other because *Batman & Robin* has features that *The Fantastic Four* lacks. If another Bad Movie Lover insisted to me that *Batman & Robin* is no better than *The Fantastic Four*, I would point out the concrete ways that *Batman & Robin* is different from *The Fantastic Four* and argue that those differences make it more valuable.

It will be helpful to deepen our comparison between good-bad movies and the avant-garde. Avant-garde art is by definition unconventional. We can't understand what makes it valuable by appealing directly to conventional standards and norms. This is exactly why many people are dismissive of it. I once saw avant-garde musician and composer John Zorn give a solo performance on a saxophone mouthpiece. It would be easy to imagine the parent of a 10-year old saxophone novice saying something about Zorn's performance like "jeez, this sounds like the unholy noise my kid makes every evening." Zorn's performance doesn't even attempt to adhere to conventional standards. To find it worthwhile, one needs a lot of context. Although it may sound random and unskilled, it is connected with his larger body of work, his methods of improvisation, and his interest in exploring unusual timbres and unconventional ways of producing sounds with musical instruments.

Zorn's performance was not good by popular standards, and yet I found it worthwhile. But *why* did I find it worthwhile? Just as there are certain reasons that I find *Batman & Robin* worthwhile but not *The Fantastic Four*, there should be certain reasons why I find John Zorn's saxophone mouthpiece experimentation worthwhile and the undisciplined warbling of a 10-year-old agonizing. It's certainly not because Zorn's performance is nice to listen to in the straightforward way that a Mozart piano concerto is. Rather, as I've indicated, I find it worthwhile because of the way it relates to Zorn's body of work and to the broader tradition of musical performance. This tradition is embodied in a network of institutions and practices: music schools, venues, performance traditions, critical forums, critical practices, and so on. This network grounds the set of norms and standards that philosopher Dominic McIver Lopes calls the "scaffolding" for aesthetic value.[1] The avant-garde is characterized by the *transgression* of received norms and standards, but those norms and standards need to be in the background or else there would be nothing to transgress.

But the avant-garde also generates its own standards and norms, orthogonal to conventional norms. Zorn's mouthpiece performance is interesting in part because of the way it relates to the standards and norms of avant-garde musical performance. Because the nature of the avant-garde is to push the perceived limits of an art form, we should expect these norms to be far less uniform and stable than conventional norms. They will shift and change as new works are produced and artists, critics, and fans discuss and debate them. There will be splinter factions and unique local scenes with distinct sets of norms and standards.

My favorite recent avant-garde film is Tsai Ming-liang's *Days*. It's two hours long and there's almost no dialogue. It alternates between long scenes showing two different men going about their daily lives. One of them is an older Taiwanese man who lives in the outskirts of Taipei, the other is a younger Laotian immigrant who lives in the urban center. We see the older man staring off into the distance in one scene, and then in another we see him struggling with neck pain. We see the younger man meticulously washing a pile of vegetables and cooking himself a meal. In the middle of the film, the younger man gives the older man an erotic massage. The film then returns to the mundane and we get more long scenes, except now we see subtle glimpses of the way the central encounter reverberates in their daily lives.

A friend who saw *Days* at a film festival told me that many audience members walked out well before it was over. Although I cringe at this display of disrespect for a film that I found very beautiful, it's not so hard to understand: mainstream standards firmly entail that more than one significant event should happen in a two hour movie. Most filmgoers are not accustomed to extended shots of someone staring off into the distance or washing vegetables. By conventional standards, it's a boring movie. It's not easy to appreciate without appropriate context, which includes familiarity with avant-garde cinema in general and the earlier works of Tsai Ming-liang in particular.

Bad Movie Love has its own network of institutions and practices, much like the avant-garde does. There are bad movie festivals, bad movie film series at repertory theaters, internet forums where Bad Movie Lovers gather, small groups of friends who regularly get together to watch bad movies, and so on. This network of practices and institutions grounds the norms and standards of bad movie love. It's *possible* to appreciate bad movies as a lonely hermit, but Bad Movie Love is so much richer when it hooks up with this larger network.

Like the avant-garde, appreciation of good-bad movies is aided by familiarity with relevant background context. I illustrated this in Chapter 5 by showing how background understanding of the context from which Cage's acting emerges (including, for instance, familiarity with German

Expressionism and his other influences) can ground a deeper appreciation of his less reputable work. Getting an informal bad movie education by participating in internet forums and consuming blogs, podcasts, and YouTube videos puts one in a much better position to appreciate bad movies. Just as most people can't expect to walk in off the street without any context and appreciate *Days*, I don't expect someone who isn't well-versed in bad movies to see the value of *Battlefield Earth*.

Much like the avant-garde, we should expect the norms and standards of Bad Movie Love to be less stable and uniform than those of the mainstream. As I've emphasized throughout the book, Bad Movie Love centrally involves developing creative forms of engagement. I want to emphasize again that these forms of engagement are not random! They are tethered to features that the movies really do have. There's a reason why *The Room* has taken off and *The Fantastic Four* hasn't.

The good-bad, the mainstream, and the avant-garde each have their own networks, but they are interconnected in various ways. Neither the avant-garde nor the good-bad could achieve the values connected with transgression of conventional norms if there were no conventional norms to transgress. To understand the value of good-bad movies, we need to see how Bad Movie Love fits into the larger project of cinephilia. First, however, we need to back up and return to the question of what makes artworks valuable in the first place.

***

I have a proposal:

- An activity of engagement is one that engages with an artwork *as* an artwork in the mode of appreciation, such as watching it, discussing it, writing about it, or curating it. Using a copy of *Don Quixote* as a dart board is not an activity of engagement in this sense, neither is reading it out loud to make fun of the way it's written.

- The value that art has *in its own right* consists in its capacity to enable valuable activities of engagement.
- The value that art has *for a person* consists in its capacity to enable valuable activities of engagement *for that person*.

According to this picture, the value of art ultimately derives from the value of the activities of engagement it enables, but there is still a sense in which art has value in its own right. Consider an analogy with food. The culinary value of a sandwich derives from the value of engaging with it: eating it, writing a review of it, debating its merits with other sandwich enthusiasts, and so on. But a sandwich only enables these valuable activities to the extent that it has features that can support them. A couple of stale slices of bread, some gross wilted lettuce, and a smear of peanut butter probably won't enable any valuable activities of engagement.

One nice thing about this proposal is that it explains the diversity of taste. We all have a different psychological makeup and life history, and so it stands to reason that we would prefer different activities. I like solving crossword puzzles, baking pies, and reading fantasy novels. I do not like solving Sudoku puzzles, knitting, or reading stock market analyses. My preferences didn't come out of nowhere: they are grounded in my particular psychological propensities and the way I've lived my life up to this point. Crossword and Sudoku puzzles are both challenging exercises, but they involve the use of different mental faculties. I find crossword puzzles enjoyable, but I find Sudoku irritating. That's just how my brain works. I find baking pies relaxing, but I find knitting tedious. I find many fantasy novels extremely entertaining, but every minute I am reading about the stock market is torture. That doesn't mean that I think other people are wrong to like Sudoku, knitting, or stock market analyses. I can easily see how someone whose brain likes words less and numbers more might prefer Sudoku, or how someone could find the repetitive trance of knitting to be more relaxing than the multistage process of baking a pie, or how someone could be fascinated by the intricacies of the stock market but entirely uninterested in the slaying of dragons. I don't think others are wrong to like those things, I just don't like them myself, and it's easy to see that this difference is explained by more basic differences in our psychological constitutions and life histories.

My proposal holds that a work of art has value in its own right to the extent that it enables valuable activities of engagement. Because different people legitimately prefer different activities, the fact that an artwork is valuable in its own right does not entail that it will be valuable for every single person. Indeed, much of what is valuable for someone else might be downright repellant for me. It's not easy to see outside one's own perspective, but sometimes I can recognize that an artwork that isn't valuable *for me* is nevertheless valuable *in its own right*, because I can recognize that it is apt to enable valuable activities of engagement for other people. I don't like listening to Elvis Costello, but I totally understand why other people do. If someone were to ask me if Elvis Costello's music is good, I would say that it is good but that it's not to my taste. On my proposal, what I'm saying here is that Elvis Costello's music enables valuable activities of engagement for other people, but not for me.

This is not to say that *anything* that *anyone* happens to find valuable thereby has value in its own right. Some people *wrongly* value certain activities of engagement. For instance, some people like white supremacist comic books. Fuck those people. They might value their own activities of engagement, but they're making a mistake. Their dipshit racist comics are actually really awful and are making their lives worse, whether they realize it or not. The question of whether an artwork has value in its own right boils down to the question of whether the activities of engagement it enables have value. They have value when they make our lives better. I don't know exactly what does and does not make for a good human life, but we can safely exclude white supremacist comic book fandom.

This thought explains the possibility of evaluating an artwork incorrectly. Suppose I watch *Memento* and I don't understand that it's in reverse chronological order, so that I'm just confused the whole time and my activity of engaging with it lacks value. I might conclude on this basis that the movie lacks value in its own right and that others are wrong to find it valuable. But suppose it actually does enable valuable activities of engagement for many people who understand the structure of the narrative. My judgment would be incorrect. I can't even justifiably deny that it's valuable *for me* as long as my evaluation is based on a mistake.

One objection to my account is that engaging with artworks that are bad (in the final sense) can be valuable. If I am very interested in the 1980s slasher movie cycle, for instance, I have good reason to explore not just the best slasher movies, but also the lousy ones. Having a fuller understanding of the various ways that a slasher movie can fall short helps me to more fully appreciate the best slasher movies as well as the larger system that contextualizes them. Suppose you've never had pizza before and the very first slice you ever try is from the legendary Brooklyn pizza parlor Di Fara. You'll surely enjoy it, but will you really be able to appreciate what's special about it? The difference between Di Fara's slice and any number of lesser slices isn't all that huge. Many lesser slices have roughly similar qualities to Di Fara. The excellence of Di Fara consists in its subtle refinement—all the little ways it excels. You wouldn't be in a position to appreciate this refinement without a basis for comparison. In the case of the slasher cycle, exploring many mediocre slasher movies puts one in the position to more fully appreciate the merits of exceptional examples like *The Burning* and *The Slumber Party Massacre*. The activity of engaging with lousy slasher movies is *instrumentally* valuable: it's valuable not for its own sake, but as a means of promoting richer engagement with *better* slasher movies and with the system that stands behind them. This does not pose a problem for my view.

One other objection to my account is that it's *too generous*. If any artwork that supports valuable activities of engagement is good, then a whole lot of artworks turn out to be good. This conclusion is not quite as provocative as it might seem, since my account also holds that only a small subset of valuable artworks will be good *for a given person*, but in any case it's a bullet I'm happy to bite. As you have probably surmised by now, I'm in favor of an open and generous attitude towards art. The intense negativity that many people are able to summon towards artworks they don't like is often more about elevating themselves above others than anything else. Call it the "narcissism of negativity." In any case, it's possible to have both an open and generous attitude towards art *and* a distinctive point of view. We can dislike something and still admit that it could be good from a different perspective. I hate Luca Guadagnino's 2018 *Suspiria* remake in the core of my being. I hereby admit that someone whose sensibility and life history are very different from mine might legitimately get a lot of value out of it. I have my reasons for disliking it, and if anyone tries to convince me that it's anywhere near as good as Argento's original, I will argue with them. But if a horror fan tells me that they have a personal connection with Guadagnino's *Suspiria* and their engagement with it has added a lot to their life, who am I to tell them that they're wrong?

***

Let's return one last time to the question of what it means when a Bad Movie Lover says that an artwork is good, bad, or good-bad. This is my final, decisive statement on the matter:

- An artwork is *good in the conventional sense* if it accords with mainstream norms and standards, and *bad in the conventional sense* if it violates them in a way that is perceived as artistically unserious.
- An artwork is *good in the final sense* if it enables valuable activities of engagement, and *bad in the final sense* if it does not enable valuable activities of engagement.
- An artwork is *good-bad* if it is good in the final sense partly in virtue of being bad in the conventional sense.

Mainstream norms and standards may fail to track actual values. It could be that many of the works that the mainstream embraces don't actually enable valuable activities of engagement, while many of the works that the mainstream rejects in fact do. But, on that note, it's finally time to say something positive about the mainstream. I discussed above the way in which networks of institutions and practices ground attendant sets of norms and standards. We can now see more clearly why this sort of institutional context is relevant to the value of art: it is the setting for valuable activities of engagement. The good-bad, the mainstream, and the avant-garde enable different activities that are valuable in different ways. The mainstream network is by far the most expansive and stable, and so acts as a firm foundation for a wide range of valuable activities, and moreover grounds the default expectations that must be in place for the good-bad and the avant-garde to register as transgressive. As John Waters said: "To know bad taste, of course, you have to have been taught the rules of the tyranny of good taste so you can yearn to break them."[2] We should expect most of the works that the mainstream prizes to be valuable in their own right. This is not to say, however, that we should expect these works to be *more* valuable than works that the mainstream rejects. Any work that grounds valuable activities of engagement is a valuable work, but some are much, much more valuable than others, and there's no reason to assume that the mainstream is picking out the best stuff.

In Chapter 2, I brought up the worry that considering movies like *The Room* to be good might unduly diminish the value of artistic achievement. Ed Wood did something special when he made *Plan 9 from Outer Space*, but there needs to be a way to find some daylight between him and Orson Welles. If *Plan 9* deserves admiration, it deserves a very different kind of admiration than *Citizen Kane*. We now have a deeper way to make this distinction. We can recognize *Citizen Kane* as a superlative masterpiece because of the way it relates to the institutional network of the mainstream. The consensus that *Citizen Kane* is one of the greatest films ever made reflects the fact that it is one of the films that define the standard of greatness. Is this a vicious circularity? No, because at the time when it was made,

Citizen Kane didn't simply adhere to existing standards. It was avant-garde art created within the studio system, combining cutting-edge technique with profound artistry. Welles' experimental orientation is the reason he was obstructed in countless ways throughout his career by those funding his work. He never played it safe; he always pushed the boundaries of the medium. The mainstream characteristically rejects the innovations of the avant-garde when it first encounters them, but without the avant-garde, the evolution of the mainstream would be stunted. I've picked on the mainstream throughout this book as a way to highlight what's special about good-bad movies. But mainstream standards aren't just boring conventions, they're a record of past revolutions. The mainstream canon reflects the rich history of the popular face of the medium. It's not perfect and it has undeniably been shaped by pernicious power hierarchies, but it is fluid and changeable and undoubtedly enables a wide range of eminently valuable activities of engagement. There's nothing wrong with the mainstream, it's just that it doesn't have a monopoly on cinematic value; there are unique and distinctive values attached to categories that fall outside it.

***

My account passes the buck from the question of the value of art to the question of the value of the activities of engagement that art enables. The question that remains for us, then, is whether the activities that bad movies enable are valuable enough to merit inclusion in a well-lived life.

Let me start out by stating clearly that I do not think that *everyone* ought to watch bad movies. There is an embarrassment of aesthetic riches in the world. There is too much great art out there to absorb in a hundred lifetimes. I argued above that we should expect different people to prefer different types of art in virtue of more basic differences in their psychological makeup and life history. Someone with a gift for language may find it rewarding to work through Joyce's *Finnegan's Wake*, while someone with a more visual orientation may legitimately prefer graphic novels. Someone whose mind craves rigorous structure may be attracted to sonnets while a more chaotic sensibility prefers free verse. I don't expect my mom to like John Zorn and she doesn't expect me to like Danielle Steel.

As I've argued, the diversity of aesthetic sensibilities in the world is a good thing. Philosopher Alexander Nehamas writes: "Imagine, if you can, a world where everyone likes, or loves, the same things, where every disagreement about beauty can be resolved. That would be a desolate, desperate world."[3] Our aesthetic preferences are an expression of *who we are*; diversity of aesthetic taste is a manifestation of more fundamental differences between us. The erasure of these differences would make for a bleak dystopian nightmare. It would be *very boring*.

We should celebrate the diversity of aesthetic sensibilities in the world rather than demanding that everyone conform to our own. I am not here to tell you that you should like bad movies (or even that you should like *any* movies). Frankly, if *everyone* liked bad movies, that would ruin it. There's no thrill of lowbrow transgression where there's no contempt from above. I'm just here to argue that bad movies *can* be a valuable ingredient in a human life—that it's OK to love bad movies.

I'll begin my final defense of Bad Movie Love by reconstructing the strongest argument I can come up with for *denying* that bad movies can be worthwhile—call it the Optimization

Argument. Then, I'll show what's wrong with this argument. Here it is:

1. Some films are considered by broad consensus to be eminently worthwhile. Call them "certified great movies."
2. People are busy. Most people won't have time to watch all of the certified great movies within their lifetime.
3. Bad movies are less worthwhile than certified great movies.
4. Time spent watching bad movies is time that could be spent watching certified great movies.

   Conclusion: There's no time for bad movies. Watch the certified greats instead.

First, we need to acknowledge that this conclusion might hold for *some* people. Imagine, for instance, a literary scholar named Professor Stuffypants who spends most of his free time reading literary fiction and listening to Bach, but likes to catch three or four movies a year, with a strong preference for art films. Given this person's sensibility, the three or four movies he takes in every year should probably be from the certified great category or the avant-garde. If I were having a water-cooler conversation with Professor Stuffypants, I would not try to talk him into checking out *Grand Isle* or *Batman & Robin*. Professor Stuffypants doesn't have time for George Clooney's bat nipples.

But the Optimization Argument fails to show that *no one* has time for bad movies. The premise I most vehemently reject, of course, is 3. I don't agree that bad movies are less worthwhile *for everyone* than certified great movies. But there is also a problem with premise 4. I will offer two objections to the Optimization Argument. The first is addressed to premise 4 and based on practical considerations, while the second is addressed to premise 3 and has the more ambitious aim of showing that engagement with the medium of film as a whole can be enhanced by Bad Movie Love.

***

Premise 4 states: "Time spent watching bad movies is time that could be spent watching certified great movies."

Before getting into detail about what this premise gets wrong, we need to introduce the concept of an "aesthetic slot." Aesthetic slots are spaces in one's life in which something aesthetic fits. Different slots have different criteria; not every activity or object fits every slot. One aesthetic slot for me is the time I spend cooking and doing other kitchen chores. In our household division of labor, this is a daily responsibility for me. Kitchen chores don't require my undivided attention, and so an aesthetic slot is created; I can engage in some further activity while I'm working in the kitchen. Movies are my preferred aesthetic domain, but they don't fit into this slot. I can't watch a movie while I cook. I need to be looking at what I'm doing and not at a screen. Instead, I can listen to music, audiobooks, or podcasts. I often choose music (dirty southern rap when I'm home alone and Taylor Swift when I'm not), but the fact that this slot is available has led me to get more interested in audiobooks. Sometimes I don't feel like music, and I've found that due to my own particular psychological makeup, it's a lot easier and more enjoyable for me to pay attention to fantasy novels than nonfiction books or podcasts, and so I often use this slot to get caught up on fantasy novels.

Another aesthetic slot for me is the stretch in the evening where I've already had a chance to wind down from the day, but I'm not yet tired. This is the time when I'm usually best capable of focusing on an artwork. Because cinema is the art form that I care about the most, I usually use this time to watch difficult movies. Sometimes my wife and I will be looking through our options for something to watch at a time when I'm not feeling at all relaxed, and she'll notice some especially demanding movie and suggest that we watch it. I'll say: "Let's save that for a day when I'm feeling more focused," and ask if there's anything lighter that she might be interested in. Difficult movies don't fit into the "I'm really stressed out right now and need something to help me relax" slot, they fit into the "alert and focused" slot. A nice, formulaic Jason Statham action flick fits much better into the "stressed out" slot.

The concept of an aesthetic slot reveals the problem with premise 4 of the Optimization Argument, which holds that time spent watching bad movies is time that could be spent watching certified great movies. Certified great movies do not necessarily fit into the same slots as bad movies. If I have a bunch of rowdy friends over and we decide to put on a movie, am I going to choose this moment to win them over to Resnais' *Last Year at Marienbad* or Chantal Akerman's *Les Rendez-vous d'Anna*? No! Definitely not! I'm going to put on *The Room* or *Troll 2*. If I just finished a big exam that I spent months studying for and feel like I'm ready to collapse, am I going to choose Resnais? No, I'm going to consume a bag of gummy bears and watch *The Core*.

The 2020 election was a very stressful time for most Americans. On Election Day, film critic Kristen Yoonsoo Kim posted a review on the film social media app Letterboxd of Adam Sandler's most recent movie *Hubie Halloween*: "got taco bell and watched for a 3rd time it's called self-care sweetie."[4] I laughed hard, because I had literally just had the *exact* same idea. For me, and evidently also for Kim, Taco Bell is comfort food and Adam Sandler movies are comfort movies. We aren't the only ones who feel this way about the Sandman. Respected director Paul Thomas Anderson once explained to a skeptical Roger Ebert why he cast Sandler in *Punch Drunk Love*:

> I wanted to work with Sandler so much, because if I've ever been kinda sad or down or whatever, I just wanna pop in an Adam Sandler movie. I love him, and he's always made me laugh. I like just about all of his movies and have always felt comfort in watching them. It's Saturday night and if I wanna watch something fun, I'm gonna watch an Adam Sandler movie. Or if I'm sad, I'm popping in an Adam Sandler movie. The last thing I would wanna do is watch *Magnolia*, you know, or *Breaking the Waves*.[5]

Comfort movies are an important slot even for many people who aren't especially keen on movies in general. Just as our favorite comfort foods are rarely doctor-approved health foods, our favorite comfort movies are rarely the certified greats. *Citizen Kane* and *The Best Years of Our Lives* are not going to help get me through Election Day anxiety; I want *Hubie Halloween*. Is it a bad movie? In the conventional sense, yes. But it's the kind of bad that soothes the soul.

Most Adam Sandler movies are paradigmatic examples of conventional badness, and his latter day output in particular has been treated as a punching bag by critics. What connection is there between the badness of these movies and their comforting quality? One thing that even detractors admit about Sandler movies is that the cast always seem like they're having a great time. These movies throw so many jokes at you that even if three out of four miss their mark you'll still be laughing most of the time. Actors get to play far out characters and do silly voices. Sandler himself is reputed to be immensely charismatic and fun to work with. These movies don't swing for the fences; they aren't trying to please critics or win awards. Part of their special magic is that because no one involved is under pressure to make a good movie, everyone is free to have fun. The audience isn't under any pressure either. Sandler doesn't demand that we think very hard or search for hidden meaning. We can just enjoy what works for us and ignore what doesn't. For me, it's the cinematic equivalent of a big, fluffy blanket (or a Crunchwrap Supreme).

***

Premise 3 of the optimization argument states: "Bad movies are less worthwhile than certified great movies."

One way to show that bad movies can be at least as worthwhile as the certified greats would be to show that the activities of engagement that bad movies enable can be at least as valuable as the activities of engagement that certified great movies enable. I don't think this is a very interesting line of argument—*of course* it's true that *some* bad movies will enable more valuable activities of engagement for *some* people than *some* of the certified critical favorites. I personally feel immensely confident that *The Room* has added a lot more to my life than *There Will Be Blood* has. QED.

A deeper and more interesting way to approach this final argument is to ask which *overall approach* to the medium of film is more promising: optimization or omnivorism. By "omnivorism" I mean a cinematic diet that includes good-bad movies alongside certified greats (and the avant-garde as well, but going into further depth about that is a topic for another book). It will be helpful to return to Susan Sontag's "Notes on 'Camp'." She writes:

> 54. The experiences of Camp are based on the great discovery that the sensibility of high culture has no monopoly upon refinement. Camp asserts that good taste is not simply good taste; that there exists, indeed, a good taste of bad taste. (Genet talks about this in Our Lady of the Flowers.) The discovery of the good taste of bad taste can be very liberating. The man who insists on high and serious pleasures is depriving himself of pleasure; he continually restricts what he can enjoy; in the constant exercise of his good taste he will eventually price himself out of the market, so to speak. Here Camp taste supervenes upon good taste as a daring and witty hedonism. It makes the man of good taste cheerful, where before he ran the risk of being chronically frustrated. It is good for the digestion.

It can't all be Resnais and Welles. The development of highly refined taste risks making us grumpy and discontent. The more we know about an art form, the more able we are to pick up on every flaw and deficiency. There's a classic image of the relentlessly negative art lover—the expert so advanced that nothing is good enough for them. I think of Bob Balaban's grumpy critic from M. Night Shyamalan's *Lady in the Water*. That the most avid lover of an art form should be the most restrictive about what they appreciate is perverse at best, and a likely recipe for a life of alienation and discontent. Bad Movie Love is one available escape from the pitfall of refinement as narrowness. It gives us the opportunity to express refinement creatively by seeing things in ways others don't, finding value in works that mainstream critics trod roughshod over, and participating in lively and distinctive affective communities.

Pauline Kael offers an exquisite argument against full-throttle optimization:

> Perhaps the single most intense pleasure of moviegoing is this non-aesthetic one of escaping from the responsibilities of having the proper responses required of us in our official (school) culture. And yet this is probably the best and most common basis for developing an aesthetic sense because responsibility to pay attention and to appreciate is anti-art, it makes us too anxious for pleasure, too bored for response. Far from supervision and official culture, in the darkness at the movies where nothing is asked of us and we are left alone, the liberation from duty and constraint allows us to develop our own aesthetic responses. Unsupervised enjoyment is probably not the only kind there is but it may feel like the only kind. Irresponsibility is part of the pleasure of all art; it is the part the schools cannot recognize.[6]

Have you ever watched through one of the lists of "the 100 greatest movies of all time" that are occasionally published by the British Film Institute, the American Film Institute, and any number of magazines and critical organizations? There's something oppressive about this sort of endeavor. One feels a sense of *obligation* to appreciate the films, as though being underwhelmed by them would be a personal failure. There is a sense of duty to have the correct response. I've been trying to like Fellini's 8 ½ for nearly thirty years and I still blame myself for the way I always lose interest after the first act. As Kael observes, this sense of duty is prone to have the opposite of its intended effect; it stunts the development of our aesthetic sense. When we go see an action movie or sit down for another round of *Hubie Halloween*, we feel free to have our *own* reactions, and this form of engagement is in some respects more conducive to the formation of a rich and distinctive sensibility than the explicitly educational enterprise of trudging through a list of certified greats.

Bad Movie Love opens the door to a huge range of idiosyncratic aesthetic projects, and these projects give us the space to develop and deploy our refinement in creative ways. While writing this book, I decided to just go right ahead and watch every single Dolph Lundgren movie I hadn't seen. When I'm finished, I'll write a blog post about my findings. Do I think every single one of these movies is independently worthwhile? Certainly not! But I find the larger project of watching them all to be immensely worthwhile. It's a perfect example of the sort of systematic engagement discussed in Chapter 3. Attending to the fine-grain nuances that distinguish Dolph's performance in *Hidden Assassin* from the one *Silent Trigger* is an unusual way to deploy refinement, but a rewarding one. When I meet someone with weird and specific expertise of this sort, I find it far more exciting than meeting someone who can recite the American Film Institute's party line on the 100 greatest movies ever made. Variety, distinctness, and idiosyncrasy make for an exciting film culture. Uniformity and presumed authority do not.

Bad movie exploration isn't about finding ways to appreciate as many bad movies as possible. Indiscriminate enjoyment is another way of being indistinct. Projects such as "watch all the Dolph Lundgren movies" also provide a valuable opportunity to develop one's ability to arrive at fine-grained judgments.

When you're *deep* in the Dolph filmography, you're in uncharted territory. Some of his more obscure DTV titles have barely been seen or reviewed by anyone. There's no default take on these movies to assent to or dissent from. One needs to find one's own path. Is *Jill the Ripper* good? Is it bad? Is it good-bad? What kind of considerations should one bring to bear when making this determination? It's a chance to lead rather than follow. By watching through the complete Dolph filmography and then writing a blog post about it, I can make a contribution to the evolution of the small affective community of Dolph Lundgren completists. What's going to happen if I write a post about the new Marvel movie or the latest Oscar winner? Not much, since the internet is already overflowing with this sort of post. To this day, the most consistently popular post on my movie blog is a listicle of 34 movies by Italian exploitation maestro Lucio Fulci. I assume this post is popular because when you search the internet for opinions on Fulci deep cuts, not a whole lot comes up. Interest in sub-mainstream esoterica is a path to more robust participation in affective communities.

If one is worried about time spent with bad movies leading to a vapid life, one should be a lot more worried about Ridicule than Love. The practices of Ridicule promote condescension, meanness, and the narrow-minded enforcement of received norms. Ridicule is a way to feel superior to others—the artist responsible for the object of one's disdain, but also that object's sincere fans. Love promotes an open, flexible, and creative aesthetic sensibility and the formation of bonds across ordinary social boundaries.

I don't mean to imply that film enthusiasts would be better off skipping the AFI's top 100. As I've argued, Bad Movie Love is enabled and enhanced by thorough familiarity with the mainstream. And, of course, many of the 100 greatest movies ever made actually are pretty great. The point is rather that narrow optimization doesn't leave appropriate space for the development of an idiosyncratic point of view, and an idiosyncratic point of view is a good thing to have, both for the person who has it and for the communities they participate in. Bad Movie Love is a path towards the development of a distinctive sensibility. Is it the only path? Of course not, but it's an especially notable one, full of opportunities for creativity and social engagement. It's also a damn good way to get over oneself and any misplaced pride one harbors in the possession of narrow and restrictive taste.

It's certainly not mandatory to love bad movies, but is it OK? I hope I've convinced you that it is.

Notes

THE GOOD, THE BAD, AND THE GOOD-BAD

1 Dyck and Johnson 2017.
2 https://fsgworkinprogress.com/2011/06/15/john-waters-on-bad-taste/
3 One worry for my view is that many people don't believe our judgments about the value of art can be correct or incorrect. In their 2019 article "An empirical investigation of guilty pleasures," philosophers Kris Goffin and Florian Cova argue that empirical studies suggest that most people don't believe that there are norms governing aesthetic value and that they don't think that judgments about the value of artworks can be correct or incorrect. Their finding isn't in direct conflict with my view, however, because people might implicitly accept a set of norms while explicitly denying that they do. I would like to see a study in which people are asked whether plot holes are a bad thing.
4 https://thefilmstage.com/tom-green-reflects-on-20-years-of-freddy-got-fingered/
5 Koshel 2016.
6 Sarkhosh and Menninghaus 2016.
7 https://www.bfi.org.uk/sight-and-sound/features/films-maudit-cursed-films-natural-history
8 Ibid.
9 https://www.filmlinc.org/daily/heavens-gate-and-the-film-maudit/
10 https://www.sensesofcinema.com/2001/jacques-rivette/rivette-2/
11 https://screencrush.com/freddy-got-fingered-15th-anniversary-appreciation/
12 https://aestheticsforbirds.com/2018/12/13/is-this-really-art-aesthetic-disagreement-and-conceptual-negotiation/
13 https://www.theguardian.com/film/series/hear-me-out
14 https://www.theguardian.com/film/2021/feb/01/godzilla-1998-roland-emmerich-monster-movie
15 Sontag 1964.

16 The origins of camp are not all fun and games. Scholar Carl Schottmiller writes: "For LGBTQ people, camp is not just about embracing irony, celebrating theatricality, valuing bad taste, and seeing the world in quotation marks. We use camp to survive in a homophobic and transphobic world that seeks to silence and destroy us. Historically, LGBTQ people use camp's irony, theatricality, parody, humor, and aestheticism to help relieve the social stigmas associated with our identities. We embrace theatricality because we've had to pass as heterosexual in order to survive, forced to learn to hide our identities through calculated self-presentation. We use irony and parody to subvert the normative gender and sex roles that define us as deviant. And we adopt an ironic and sarcastic bitter wit in order to neutralize the sting of homophobia and transphobia. Gallows humor gives us a way to laugh at and mock our stigmatized identities. For LGBTQ people, Camp has been one of our most powerful subcultural practices." https://aestheticsforbirds.com/2019/05/06/what-is-camp-five-scholars-discuss-sontag-the-met-gala-and-camps-queer-origins/#schottmiller

17 https://www.statista.com/statistics/187300/box-office-market-share-of-disney-in-north-america-since-2000/

18 https://collider.com/edgar-wright-ant-man-production-problems-explained/

19 https://variety.com/2018/film/features/solo-a-star-wars-story-directors-reshoots-ron-howard-1202817841/

20 https://birthmoviesdeath.com/2015/03/16/the-critical-transfoormation-of-alfred-hitchcocks-vertigo

ARTISTS' INTENTIONS AND BAD MOVIE GREATNESS

1 Hoberman 1980, 8.

2 Carroll 2001, 177–8.

3 Ibid.

A BEAUTIFUL RAINBOW OF BADNESS

1 Singleton 2019.

2 https://www.rogerebert.com/reviews/battlefield-earth-2000

3 Ibid.

4 https://illgetdrivethru.com/2020/07/31/why-is-batman-robin-considered-the-worst-batman-movie/

5 https://www.advocate.com/commentary/2020/6/24/joel-schumacher-reluctant-and-conflicted-gay-trailblazer

6 https://www.vice.com/en/article/xw8vpk/twenty-years-later-joel-schumacher-is-very-sorry-about-batman-and-robin
7 Quoted in https://www.denofgeek.com/movies/batman-forever-why-the-batsuit-had-nipples/
8 https://twitter.com/driverminnie/status/1275219191323217920
9 Anecdotes in this paragraph are from the 2014 documentary *Electric Boogaloo: The Wild, Untold Story of Cannon Films*.
10 Impastato 1994, 38.
11 https://film.avclub.com/today-s-best-action-directors-aren-t-working-in-hollywo-1798241342
12 Kael 1969, 91–2.
13 Roberts 1990, 150–1.
14 https://die-hard-scenario.fandom.com/wiki/Die_Hard_scenario_Wiki
15 Comic books are another great example. Cf., Cowling and Cray 2022, section 8.5. Thanks to Ley Cray for recommending Roberts on junk fiction to me.
16 https://www.filmcomment.com/blog/review-universal-soldier-day-of-reckoning-jean-claude-van-damme/
17 https://www.usatoday.com/story/life/movies/2012/11/29/universal-soldier-reckoning-review/1715207/?utm_source=feedburner&utm_medium=feed&utm_campaign=Feed%3A+UsatodaycomMovies-TopStories+%28USATODAY+-+Movies+Top+Stories%29
18 Kael 1969, 115.
19 https://www.nytimes.com/1989/04/21/movies/review-film-dolph-lundgren-in-red-scorpion.html

TASTE AND *TWILIGHT*

1 Pinkowitz 2011.
2 Bourdieu, 1979, 56.
3 Wilson 2007, 92–3.
4 https://www.straight.com/article-172132/twilight
5 https://www.rottentomatoes.com/m/twilight/reviews?type=&sort=&page=5
6 Riggle 2017, 45.
7 Cohen 1999a, 28.
8 Cohen 1993, 155.
9 Cohen 1999b, 41.
10 Ibid.

11 Cowling and Cray 2022, 198.
12 https://en.wikipedia.org/wiki/Mystery_Science_Theater_3000#Reactions_by_those_parodied

NICOLAS CAGE AND THE LIMITS OF THE CRITICAL IMAGINATION

1 https://www.salon.com/2019/12/03/grand-isle-review-nicolas-cage/
2 Gibb 2015, 23.
3 https://www.nytimes.com/interactive/2019/08/07/magazine/nicolas-cage-interview.html
4 https://time.com/3973963/nicolas-cage-interview/
5 https://www.washingtonpost.com/wp-srv/style/longterm/movies/videos/vampireskissrhinson_a0a93e.htm
6 Kael 1991, 812.
7 https://jonathanrosenbaum.net/1989/06/vampire-s-kiss/
8 https://www.rogerebert.com/reviews/great-movie-adaptation-2002
9 https://www.theringer.com/movies/2019/6/13/18663380/nicolas-cage-vampires-kiss-breakout-performance-30-years
10 https://www.interviewmagazine.com/film/nicolas-cage-marilyn-manson-in-conversation
11 Quoted in https://www.nytimes.com/2014/11/26/arts/television/whats-on-tv-wednesday.html.
12 https://www.rogerebert.com/interviews/bringing-out-scorsese
13 https://www.nytimes.com/interactive/2019/08/07/magazine/nicolas-cage-interview.html
14 https://www.interviewmagazine.com/film/nicolas-cage-marilyn-manson-in-conversation
15 https://tucson.com/lifestyles/nothing-in-this-film-works-except-fiery-skull/article_a6096687-47a1-5dd6-be17-165947891f7c.html
16 https://www.bendsource.com/bend/nicky-paycheck-once-again-cage-is-the-odd-man-out-in-drive-angry/Content?oid=2137359
17 https://fivethirtyeight.com/features/the-five-types-of-nicolas-cage-movies/
18 https://www.gamesradar.com/movies-to-watch-24-february-2017/
19 https://www.flickeringmyth.com/2017/01/movie-review-arsenal-2017/
20 https://wegotthiscovered.com/movies/rage-review-nicolas-cage/
21 https://www.latimes.com/entertainment/movies/la-et-mn-rage-review-20140711-story.html

22 https://spectrumculture.com/2014/07/14/rage-2/
23 https://www.indiewire.com/2018/02/nicolas-cage-looking-glass-review-1201929810/
24 https://www.oneguysopinion.com/looking-glass/
25 http://cinemalogue.com/2018/02/16/capsule-reviews-feb-16/
26 https://saportareport.com/joe-nicholas-cage-reminds-us-that-he-really-is-a-fine-actor/
27 https://www.vulture.com/2014/04/nicolas-cage-doesnt-need-a-mcconaissance.html
28 https://www.reddit.com/r/movies/comments/ffyvir/nicolas_cage_made_29_directtovideo_movies
29 https://www.avclub.com/foolhardy-redditor-reviews-every-direct-to-video-nic-ca-1842239187
30 https://www.nytimes.com/interactive/2019/08/07/magazine/nicolas-cage-interview.html
31 https://www.newsreview.com/sacramento/content/snrs-best-and-worst-films-of-2018/27507755/
32 Gibb 2015, 5.
33 https://www.flickfilosopher.com/2006/09/the-wicker-man-review.html
34 http://www.threemoviebuffs.com/review/wickerman.html
35 https://www.reelviews.net/reelviews/wicker-man-the
36 https://www.nytimes.com/interactive/2019/08/07/magazine/nicolas-cage-interview.html
37 https://www.nytimes.com/interactive/2019/08/07/magazine/nicolas-cage-interview.html
38 https://labuzamovies.com/2013/06/03/expressive-esoterica-in-the-21st-century-or-what-is-vulgar-auteurism/

BAD MOVIES AND THE GOOD LIFE

1 Lopes 2018, 110 ff.
2 https://fsgworkinprogress.com/2011/06/15/john-waters-on-bad-taste/
3 Nehamas 2010, 83.
4 https://letterboxd.com/kristenyoonsoo/film/hubie-halloween/2/
5 https://www.rogerebert.com/interviews/love-at-first-sight
6 Kael 1969, 104.

References

Bourdieu, Pierre. 1979. *Distinction: A Social Critique of the Judgment of Taste*. Translated by Richard Nice. Cambridge: Harvard University Press.

Carroll, Noël. 2001. *Beyond Aesthetics: Philosophical Essays*. New York: Cambridge University Press.

Cohen, Ted. 1993. "High and low thinking about high and low art." *Journal of Aesthetics and Art Criticism*. 51 (2): 151–6.

Cohen, Ted. 1999a. *Jokes: Philosophical Thoughts on Joking Matters*. Chicago: University of Chicago Press.

Cohen, Ted. 1999b. "High and low art, and high and low audiences." *Journal of Aesthetics and Art Criticism*. 57 (2): 137–43.

Cowling, Sam and Wesley D. Cray. 2022. *Philosophy of Comics: An Introduction*. London: Bloomsbury.

Dyck, John and Matt Johnson. 2017. "Appreciating bad art." *Journal of Value Inquiry*. 51: 279–92.

Gibb, Lindsay. 2015. *National Treasure: Nicolas Cage*. Toronto: ECW Press.

Goffin, Kris and Florian Cova. 2019. "An empirical investigation of guilty pleasures." *Philosophical Psychology*. 32 (7): 1129–55.

Hagendorf, Colin Atrophy. *Slice Harvester: A Memoir in Pizza*. New York: Simon & Schuster.

Hoberman, J. 1980. "Bad movies." *Film Comment*. 16 (4): 7–12.

Hoberman, J. 2021. "No success like failure – a natural history of the film maudit." *Sight and Sound*. https://www.bfi.org.uk/sight-and-sound/features/films-maudit-cursed-films-natural-history.

Impastato, David. 1994. "Godard's 'Lear'... Why is it so bad?" *Shakespeare Bulletin*. 12 (3): 38–41.

Jancovich, Mark. 2002. "Cult fictions: Cult movies, subcultural capital and the production of cultural distinctions." *Cultural Studies*. 16 (2): 306–22.

Kael, Pauline. 1969. "Trash, art, and the movies." Reprinted (1970) in *Going Steady: Film Writings 1968–1969*. Boston: Little Brown and Company.

Kael, Pauline. 1991. 5001 *Nights at the Movies* (Expanded Edition). New York: Holt Paperbacks.

Koshel, Frank. 2016. *Life Experience: Freddy Got Fingered As Neo-Surrealist Masterpiece* (master's thesis). https://academicworks.cuny.edu/cgi/ viewcontent.cgi?article=2374&context=gc_etds

Lopes, Dominic McIver. 2018. *Being for Beauty: Aesthetic Agency and Value*. Oxford: Oxford University Press.

Medved, Harry, Michael Medved and Randy Lowel. 1978. *The Fifty Worst Films of All Time (and How They Got That Way)*. New York: Warner Books.

Nehamas, Alexander. 2010. *Only a Promise of Happiness: The Place of Beauty in a World of Art*. Princeton: Princeton University Press.

Pinkowitz, Jacqueline Marie. 2011. "'The rabid fans that take [Twilight] much too seriously': The construction and rejection of excess in *Twilight* antifandom." *Transformative Works and Cultures*. 7.

Riggle, Nick. 2017. *On Being Awesome: A Unified Theory of How Not to Suck*. London: Penguin Books.

Roberts, Thomas J. 1990. *An Aesthetics of Junk Fiction*. Athens: University of Georgia Press.

Sarkhosh, Keyvan and Winfried Menninghaus. 2016. "Enjoying trash films: Underlying features, viewing stances, and experiential response dimensions." *Poetics*. 57: 40–54.

Sestero, Greg and Tom Bissell. 2013. *The Disaster Artist: My Life Inside The Room, The Greatest Bad Movie Ever Made*. New York: Simon & Schuster.

Singleton, Daniel. 2019. "The bad auteur(ist): Authentic failure and failed authenticity in Tim Burton's *Ed Wood*." *Quarterly Review of Film and Video*. 36 (5): 441–4.

Sontag, Susan. 1964. "Notes on 'Camp'." Reprinted (1966) in *Against Interpretation*. New York: Farrar, Straus, & Giroux.

Wilson, Carl. 2007. *Let's Talk About Love: A Journey to the End of Taste*. New York: Continuum.

Index

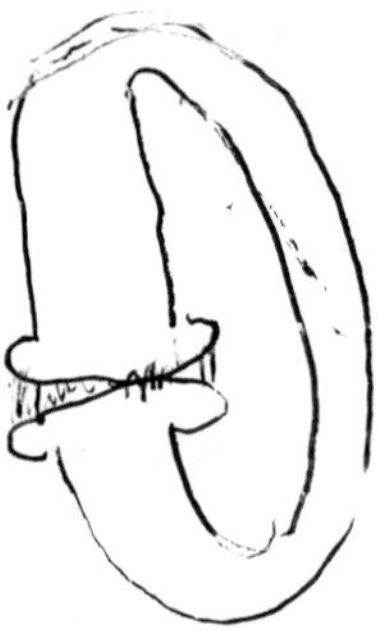